THE HIDDEN SECRETS AND STORIES OF WALT DISNEY WORLD

D1191903

MIKE FOX

ISBN-13: 978-1733598347

V3 – CS - 060120

To Elliott.

Welcome to the planet.

Next stop...Walt Disney World!

THE HIDDEN SECRETS
& STORIES OF
WALT DISNEY WORLD

"It's hard to teach an old mouse new tricks...but this book provides hours of surprises for the most knowledgeable of Disney fans."

– Peter Whitehead - **Walt Disney Hometown Museum**

Includes Secrets and Photos Not Found in Any Other Disney Books, Articles or Web Sites

Over 500 WDW Secrets
– With More Than 400 Photos!

(You'll find more than just facts or trivia)

Yes, Cinderella Castle may be 189' high, the distance around World Showcase Lagoon is 1.2 miles, and Disney's Animal Kingdom opened on April 22, 1998, but those aren't the kind of "secrets" you'll find here. Instead, you'll discover fascinating secrets and stories that reflect interviews with Disney Legends, Imagineers, and other Disney notables, as well as hundreds of hours of research involving untold trips to Walt Disney World and the Walt Disney Family Museum, poring over books, vintage materials, and obscure sources, procuring rare Disney items, and so much more, **all complete with photos**!

And now all of that is yours!

- Learn where to find Madame Leota, who appears in a mirror...*outside the Haunted Mansion*

- Discover why the Disney Imagineers chose the design they used for the gas street lamps of Main Street, U.S.A. – Told here for the very first time

- Learn of some of the tiniest overlooked details that the Imagineers have hidden in Disney's Animal Kingdom – Revealed here for the first time

- Discover the hidden tribute to the Imagineers who created Pandora

- Journey to Star Wars: Galaxy's Edge and discover the hidden tribute to Mardji, an elephant that played a Bantha in *Star Wars: A New Hope*

- Read the amazing story of how one lucky guest was called upon by Disney to help create an attraction – Published here for the very first time

- Learn the contents of the message being sent in the telegraph scene of Spaceship Earth – Revealed here for the first time ever

- Discover how the Imagineers designed and built Liberty Square so it reflects a chronological walk through America's Colonial history

- Discover where you can find over 100 Hidden Mickeys all in one place

- See photos of the smallest and largest Hidden Mickeys in all of Walt Disney World Resort

- Discover exactly where to find the special Hidden Mickey that appears only once a year

- Find out the meaning behind the items hidden in the rafters at Tom Sawyer Island – Revealed for the very first time

- Learn how YOU can pilot the Liberty Belle riverboat and receive your own pilot's license souvenir

- Learn about the first-ever revealed connection between the colorful Mutoscopes of Main Street, U.S.A and a young 12 year-old Walt Disney

- Now learn for the first time about the ominous warning at the entrance to the Haunted Mansion that 99% of guests miss

- Read the never-before-published story of the Imagineers' Frontierland tribute to A.C. Dietz...who lived 100 years before Disneyland and WDW

- And many, many more! **Over 500** magical secrets arranged as a fun tour throughout the parks

- **Complete with more than 400 photos!**

Follow
Disney-Secrets Online

On the Web:
www.Disney-Secrets.com

On Twitter:
@149G22

On Facebook:
www.Facebook.com/Disney-Secrets
(Look for the icon above)

CONTENTS

INTRODUCTION

Walt Disney World is a grand stage upon which a story of magic, fantasy and enchantment plays out for guests from around the world each and every day. Cast Members perform, attractions entertain, parades delight, and fireworks fill the night sky as guests young and old watch with wide-eyed wonder and amazement while the story unfolds all around them. But unknown to many, separate and oftentimes whimsical hidden stories play out right alongside the main act, and these stories make up *The Hidden Secrets & Stories of Walt Disney World.*

With your first visits to the parks, it's all about the attractions...as it should be. There are pirate ships to sail, characters to meet, nations to wander, and an entire galaxy to explore. But just beyond that is an all new world of discovery...one which the Disney Imagineers have purposely hidden with the hopes you'll find it.

Want to pilot the grand Liberty Square riverboat? All you have to do is ask. Want to have Main Street, U.S.A. all to yourself? Now you can. That wall of countless animal faces in Disney's Animal Kingdom? Look closer and you'll see it holds over 100 small Hidden Mickeys. And that ominous warning that 99% of guests miss as they are entering the Haunted Mansion? Now that you're aware, you'd better take heed!

And it all came to be with perhaps Walt Disney World's biggest secret of all, it's beginning...

The Beginning of Walt Disney World

"Believe me, it's the most exciting and challenging assignment we have ever tackled at Walt Disney Productions."

Walt Disney speaking about Walt Disney World

THE BEGINNING

The history of Walt Disney World reads like a suspense novel; an exciting story of intrigue, mystery, false identities and real estate deals cloaked in secrecy, but it's also a story of vision, hope, promise and great success.

Walt Disney World Resort was born out of Walt Disney's dream to bring the magic of Disneyland to more guests from around the world and to realize his vision of creating a Community of Tomorrow, a harmonious city that embraced the environment, technology and American values which Walt treasured so much.

While dedicated on October 1, 1971, Walt Disney World actually began in 1958 with Walt's commission of Economics Research Associates to study and recommend a location on the East Coast which would allow him to duplicate the success of Disneyland and realize his dream of creating a Community of Tomorrow. Walt was very clear on the criteria for the site . . . it had to have sunny and warm weather year-round, it had to be readily accessible by millions of guests and, perhaps most importantly, it had to have plenty of inexpensive land available for purchase so Walt could protect his new park from the same kind of urban blight that had come to encroach upon Disneyland.

While Disneyland was very successful at bringing magic and memories to the lives of millions of guests and their families, Walt had always been disappointed by how developers and promoters had ringed the park with a tawdry collection of hotels, restaurants and other businesses concerned more about revenue than creating a magical guest experience. With plenty of acreage at his new site, Walt could control the guest experience outside the parks and maintain the magic of his *new* Disneyland.

In 1959 Palm Beach, Florida was recommended for the new Disney World park over other sites, including Niagara Falls, St. Louis and a site between Washington D.C. and Baltimore. Unfortunately, negotiations over 12,000 acres in North Palm Beach fell through, and a second survey was commissioned to find an alternate site. This suited Walt as he felt the Palm Beach site, while located near water, was subject to humid weather and the full force of hurricanes. Walt declared his desire to have the park be located inland and two other sites were recommended; Ocala and Orlando.

In November of 1963, Walt flew to Florida with Joe Potter, Buzz Price, Jack Sayers, Donn Tatum and Card Walker to make a final decision on the new park's specific location. After flying over the coastline, as well as the swamps and forests of central Florida, Walt returned home with his final decision. The new Disneyland and Community of Tomorrow was to be located in central Florida near Orlando.

A MAGICAL SECRET

With Walt's decision, plans were put into high gear and a strategy was developed to make sure Walt could secure enough property for his new project. It was important to keep word of his decision and the ensuing land purchases secret, for if anyone knew Walt Disney was buying land to create a new Disneyland near Orlando, the price per acre would skyrocket overnight. The key now was to buy all of the land, over 27,000 acres, without arousing suspicion.

In February of 1964, after a final review by Roy Disney, Walt gave the go ahead to begin acquiring land. Operating under such company names as Reedy Creek Ranch Corporation, Bay Lake Properties, Latin-America Development and Management Corporation, and other mysterious names, Walt Disney began buying thousands of acres of land.

In time, word of major land buys began to filter through the community and rumors began to fly. Many believed a large company was looking to build a major manufacturing or headquarters site, and, given the site's proximity to Cape Canaveral and the Kennedy Space Center, speculation focused heavily on aerospace companies, including Boeing, McDonnell Aircraft, Douglas Aviation, Lockheed and others. In addition, companies including Ford, Volkswagen, Chrysler and even Howard Hughes were considered as candidates. Interestingly, some even suspected Walt Disney was buying property for an "East Coast Disneyland."

In October of 1965, after a long and tedious process, Walt had purchased nearly all of the land he needed and more . . . 27,258 acres at a price of a little over $5,000,000. More and more people were now convinced it was Walt Disney who was buying the land, and on October 24th, the Orlando Sentinel, as a result of the work of Reporter Emily Bavar, reported in a headline, "We Say It's Disney." With that, Walt made the decision to announce his plans for Florida. On November 15th, 1965, Florida's Governor, Haydon Burns, introduced Walt Disney at a press conference as, "the man of the decade, who will bring a new world of entertainment, pleasure and economic development to the State of Florida."

Walt explained to all those present . . . *"This is the biggest thing we've ever tackled. I might, for the benefit of the press, explain that my brother and I have been together in our business for forty-two years now. He's my big brother, and he's the one that when I was a little fellow I used to go to with some of my wild ideas, and he'd either straighten me out or put me on the right path - or if he didn't agree with me, I'd work on it for years until I got him to agree with me. But I must say that we've had our problems that way, and that's been the proper balance that we've been needing in our organization . . . In this project, I'd just like to say that I didn't have to work very hard on him.*

He was with me from the start. Now whether that's good or bad, I don't know."

"I would like to be part of building a model community, a City of Tomorrow, you might say, because I don't believe in going out to this extreme blue-sky stuff that some architects do. I believe that people still want to live like human beings. There's a lot of things that could be done. I'm not against the automobile, but I just feel that the automobile has moved into communities too much. I feel that you can design so that the automobile is there, but still put people back as pedestrians again, you see. I'd love to work on a project like that. Also, I mean, in the way of schools, facilities for the community, community entertainments and life. I'd love to be part of building up a school of tomorrow . . . This might become a pilot operation for the teaching age - to go out across the country and across the world. The great problem of today is the one of teaching."

THE WORLD BEGINS

Walt felt that the tested concepts and technologies of Disneyland had proven very successful, and the success in Anaheim would readily translate to Florida. As a result, he wanted to focus his attention on his new Community of Tomorrow. *"The most exciting, and by far the most important part of our Florida project. In fact, the heart of everything we'll be doing in Disney World – will be our Experimental Prototype Community of Tomorrow. We call it EPCOT. EPCOT will take its cues from the new ideas and new technologies that are now emerging from the creative centers of American industry. It will be a community of tomorrow that will never be completed, but will always be introducing and demonstrating and testing new materials and new systems. And EPCOT will always be a showcase to the world for the ingenuity and imagination of American free enterprise."*

Walt formed a committee to oversee the planning for what was to become Disney World. Consisting of himself, Marvin

Davis and Joe Potter, the planning committee was set up under WED Enterprises, an organization Walt had created in 1952 to oversee the development and construction of Disneyland. In short order, this team and others pushed forward with engineering and design analysis, site preparation plans, infrastructure planning, project PR and even legislative proposals to establish the authority of the Reedy Creek Improvement District as a quasi-governmental entity to oversee this new city and two new municipalities.

Over the ensuing months, Walt threw himself into the Florida project with his creative enthusiasm and visionary genius, with extra attention being paid to his Community of Tomorrow. Sadly, however, Walt's health took a turn for the worse, and on December 15, 1966, a little over one year after announcing his plans for Disney World and Epcot, Walt Disney passed away.

With the passing of Walt Disney, Roy Disney, at the age of 73, put aside his retirement plans and took the lead in developing Disney World, and in the fall of 1967, site preparation began. As a tribute to his brother, Roy declared that the official name of the Florida project would now be recognized as Walt Disney World. *"Everybody knows the Ford car, but not everybody knows it was Henry Ford who started it all. It's going to be Walt Disney World, so people will always know this was Walt's dream."*

Because swampland and forests were chosen as the site of Walt Disney World, one of the first projects was to drain and control the swampland for construction without seriously impacting the area's fragile ecosystem, something which was very important to Walt Disney. To achieve this, 55 miles of canals and levees were constructed along natural contour lines to efficiently control the delicate natural water systems and preserve the environment.

CONSTRUCTING WALT DISNEY WORLD

The construction of Walt Disney World was designed to occur in phases. Phase One focused on providing the key initial vacation amenities required to open the park and provide guests with the Disney experience they had come to expect, including the Magic Kingdom, five resort hotels, golfing and other activities and necessary park infrastructure.

Walt's first choice for the new Magic Kingdom was directly west of Bay Lake, the largest natural body of water on the property. However, tests showed that the land at this site was unsuitable for construction, so the decision was made to excavate this area and fill it with water, thus creating a new body of water, known as the Seven Seas Lagoon. Today, the Seven Seas Lagoon provides a stunning transition for guests as they journey to and from The Magic Kingdom via boat or monorail, thus achieving Walt's desire to maintain the magic well beyond the entrance gates of his new park.

One of the first construction objectives was to raise the height of the land for the new Magic Kingdom by 14 feet. Walt desired to have not only the park itself, but also its main focal point, Cinderella Castle, sit higher than the surrounding property to give it a sense of visual presence. In addition, raising the park was necessary in order to include the "utilidors" and service infrastructure underneath the park, which allowed cast members and service crews to move from location to location within the park without being visible to the guests "on stage." This was borne of Walt's frustration at seeing a Disneyland cast member in western attire walking through Tomorrowland one day while on his way from costuming to his work station. Walt felt this visual conflict of appearance confused guests and detracted from the guests' experience and the magic of Disneyland. From this, Walt came up with the idea of building utility corridors, or utilidors, under the Magic Kingdom, which would allow cast members to move about unseen by guests, as well as provide a means to move trash, water, laundry, etc. all out of view.

With much of the below ground infrastructure completed, construction of the Magic Kingdom began in late 1969, starting with Main Street, U.S.A. and Cinderella Castle. While Imagineers could draw upon Disneyland's Main Street, U.S.A. for both inspiration and direction, the construction of a large 189 foot high castle that captured the magic of a classic Disney animated feature film was entirely new for them. Drawing inspiration from Disney Legend Herbert Ryman's work in designing the castle, as well as from the animated feature Cinderella and several real-life French castles, including Chateau de Chambord, Chateau de Chenonceau and Chateau d'Usse, Imagineers completed this work of art and architecture in July of 1971, only three months before the park opened.

On October 1, 1971, Roy Disney opened Walt Disney World and The Magic Kingdom to the delight of countless millions around the world, both young and old. The park's inauguration included Roy's moving dedication, which can be found today on a bronze plaque on Main Street, U.S.A.:

"Walt Disney World is a tribute to the philosophy and life of Walter Elias Disney . . . and to the talents, the dedication, and the loyalty of the entire Disney organization that made Walt Disney's dream come true. May Walt Disney World bring Joy and Inspiration and New Knowledge to all who come to this happy place . . . a Magic Kingdom where the young at heart of all ages can laugh and play and learn - together."

During Walt Disney World's first year, over 10 million guests visited the park, and today over one billion guests from around the world have enjoyed its exciting attractions, thrilling stories and countless magical moments.

www.Disney-Secrets.com

CHAPTER TWO

SECRETS OF THE MAGIC KINGDOM

"Here in Florida, we have something special we never enjoyed at Disneyland...the blessing of size. There's enough land here to hold all the ideas and plans we can possibly imagine."

- Walt Disney

WELCOME!

We begin our tour of the hidden secrets and stories of Walt Disney World at the Magic Kingdom before continuing on to the rest of the parks.

As you make your way through the Magic Kingdom, you'll walk past, over and even through countless secrets and story elements just waiting to be discovered. Hidden Mickeys and cryptic messages hide in plain sight, while touching tributes and special guest experiences await only those who are "in the know." In the pages that follow, you'll discover the secrets of the Magic Kingdom to see and experience the park in an all new way! Let's begin at the entrance...

THE GANG SAYS "HELLO"

Sleep in and you'll miss this first secret. Every morning, Mickey Mouse, Minnie Mouse, Donald Duck, Goofy and the rest of the Disney character gang arrive aboard the grand Lilly Belle steam engine at the Main Street Railroad Station just prior to the opening of the Magic Kingdom to greet guests and welcome them to another day of wonder, magic and memories.

www.Disney-Secrets.com

YOUR ONLY CHANCE OF THE DAY

If you want to get a classic photo of the train engine, cars and Disney characters positioned directly in front of the Main Street Railroad Station, then the opening ceremony is the time to do it. Why? Because this is the one and only time during the day in which the engine is stopped directly in front of the station, complete with your favorite characters. All throughout the rest of the day it pulls forward and comes to a stop *just beyond* the station to allow guests to safely board the passenger cars.

LEARN ALL ABOUT
THE LOCOMOTIVES OF THE
WALT DISNEY WORLD RAILROAD

For much of his life, the world of railroading was of great interest to Walt Disney, and for many guests The Walt Disney World Railroad holds the same kind of allure. If you're a fan of the trains that ply the tracks at the Magic Kingdom, then be sure to visit the first floor of the Main Street Railroad Station. Here, you can learn all about each of the four locomotives of the railroad, as well as see artifacts which depict just a small portion of the fascinating history of railroading in America.

www.Disney-Secrets.com

THE TICKET OFFICE

Step outside the train station and find the Ticket Office window on the second floor. Peer inside and you'll find an interesting collection of vintage railroad items, including freight bills, oil cans, luggage tags and a genuine copy of Harper's Weekly from August 2, 1862. In addition, there on the wall are two old photos of historic steam engines. Study these closely, and you may find they look familiar.

The framed photo on the bottom is of the Magic Kingdom's Lilly Belle steam engine prior to her original refurbishment. Built in September of 1928 by Baldwin Locomotive Works, this grand engine was discovered by Roger Broggie and his team in the state of Yucatan in Mexico and refurbished in time for the Magic Kingdom's opening day on October 1, 1971.

Above the photo of the Lilly Belle is an image of an old steam engine sitting on rails at a sugar cane plantation in Louisiana. Though rusted and in a state of disrepair, this engine would be restored to become the bright and shiny Fred Gurley, which plys the tracks today at Disneyland in California.

OLD TO NEW CHOO CHOO

The oldest train engine is also the newest! From the Walt Disney Company...

"Built in 1916, almost a decade earlier than the Walter E. Disney and Roger E. Broggie train engines, the Roy O. Disney is the only steam engine that did not debut at the Magic Kingdom's opening on October 1, 1971. It was not until December of that year that it joined its three fellow passenger trains on the tracks at the Walt Disney World

Railroad. The new train missed the Magic Kingdom's opening date by two months, and instead made the perfect Christmas gift for the new park: Roy O. Disney - Number 4."

CLICKS AND CLACKS
AT THE TRACKS

After entering the park, stop and listen at the Main Street Railroad Station. Do you hear the telegraph working? That's the Morse Code rendition of a portion of Walt Disney's opening day speech at Disneyland on July 17, 1955, and it plays all throughout the day.

Note: Those guests who are skilled at understanding Morse Code may find the message tapped here to be unrecognizable. Why? Because the Imagineers, in their attention to detail, created it in the period specific "American Morse", also known as "Railroad Morse", which preceded today's globally recognized "International Morse Code."

TOUR THE RAILROAD

Are you a big fan of the Walt Disney World Railroad? Want a behind the scenes look at what goes into maintaining the locomotives and preparing them for use each day at the Magic Kingdom? Then you're in luck! Disney offers the 3-hour *The Magic Behind Our Steam Trains* tour every day, except Friday and Sunday. Call 407-939-8687 to learn more and to make reservations.

PAUSE FOR 100 YEARS

The Magic Kingdom awaits, but before you step into this magical world, take a moment to climb the stairs of the Main Street Railroad Station and take a look inside. It's easy to dismiss it as simply an old railroad station from the turn of the last century, but pause and consider that the entire building was constructed in 1971! The Imagineers successfully captured the look, feel and essence of another era, one which ties seamlessly with turn-of-the-20th-century Main Street, U.S.A.

CRANK UP THE ACTION

Here's a secret that takes you back to another time for some old-fashioned fun, all for only a penny.

While in the Main Street Railroad Station, you'll find some antique cast iron "Clamshell" mutoscopes. Introduced in 1895, the mutoscope was one of the most popular machines in penny arcades across the country and provided customers with a form of moving entertainment before the era of motion pictures. Though they were wildly popular in their day, mutoscopes such as these are extremely rare now. If you were to find one, chances are it wouldn't work, so this is truly a once-in-a-lifetime opportunity to see this unique form of turn-of-the-20th-century entertainment. Simply drop in a penny, peek into the viewer and turn the crank to watch an exciting, albeit brief, old movie.

Note: It's surprising to discover that the mutoscope, while patented by Herman Casler in 1894, was invented by none other than Winsor McCay, who played an important role in the life of Walt Disney.  Inside each machine are over 800 cards, each of which is printed with a photographic image from approximately 50 feet of film, and these cards "flip" by rapidly as the user turns the crank. This is a process which is very similar to that of animated film, in which countless animated stills appear in rapid succession so as to give the illusion of fluid movement. It's only logical that Winsor McCay would go on to develop and publish in 1914 what is considered to be the very first cartoon featuring an animated character, titled *Gertie the Dinosaur.* This is the film that is recognized by The Walt Disney Company as having played an important role in inspiring a young 12 year-old Walt Disney to become an animator. By the way, remember Gertie's name when you're at Echo Lake at Disney's Hollywood Studios.

WHO KNOWS THE ROSE?

Now take a look at the floor of the train station. There in the middle is a large compass rose, which is only fitting for a train station from which guests disembark for distant lands. Stand in the middle of this compass rose and, using the compass app on your phone,  discover that Main Street, U.S.A. was built to perfectly align north and south.

A NOTE OF COINCIDENCE

Nearby, you'll find a beautifully restored orchestrion. Built in 1927 by the J.P. Seeburg Piano Company, its wooden cabinet is filled with numerous instruments, including a piano, a mandolin, a xylophone, castanets, a tambourine and more, all of which come to life to play old-fashioned music from the days of Steamboat Willie. Of note is that two employees of the J.P. Seeburg Company, Oscar Nelson and Peder Wiggen, struck out on their own in 1922 to start their own business. Observant guests will recognize an orchestrion similar to this model can be found inside the Silver Spurs Mercantile in Disneyland, and this was made by none other than the new Nelson-Wiggen Piano Company.

A MAGICAL VIEW

Before you descend the stairs back to Town Square, take in the view of Main Street, U.S.A. from the balcony. This is perhaps one of the finest views of Cinderella Castle you'll find in the entire park and an excellent place from which to view Halloween, Christmas and other seasonal decorations.

A Subtle Trick of the Eye

You probably didn't notice as you approached the Magic Kingdom, but you were actually ascending a gradual slope as you walked. The ground you're standing on throughout the park is 14' higher than its original elevation. This is because Disney Imagineers needed to raise the "base" of the Magic Kingdom for two reasons; one was to hide the ten-foot high, twelve-foot wide corridors, or "Utilidors", which run beneath the park so as to allow for the unseen movement of supplies, materials and Cast Members during the day, and the other was to keep the park from flooding. The land upon which all of Walt Disney World Resort sits was semi-swampland when Walt bought it, so the Imagineers dug fill material from the bottom of a small lake in front of the Magic Kingdom and deposited it where you're now standing. This not only solved the swamp problem, but it also created the beautiful Seven Seas Lagoon you see today!

You're In The Movies

Unknown by many, Walt Disney designed the entrance to the Magic Kingdom to reveal itself as if you were walking into the opening of a Disney movie.

As you pass under the Main Street Railroad Station, you'll notice movie posters on the walls promoting the coming attractions in much the same way as movie trailers do in a theater. In this case, they promote the attractions you're about to experience during your day in the park. Next, the curtain "rises" as you emerge from the tunnels and take in the "opening act" of Town Square and Main Street, U.S.A. The story that is the Magic Kingdom begins to unfold as music fills the air, the scene reveals itself and the characters appear. Nearby is an old-fashioned popcorn cart. Always staged right by the entrance to Town Square, it offers fresh popped theater popcorn as a tasty treat. Next, as you begin to walk down Main Street, U.S.A., you'll see the "opening credits" displayed on the windows of the second and third stories of the building facades. These "actors" are the names of the Disney Imagineers, Executives, Cast Members and others who played an important role in the creation of Walt Disney World and all the magic you're about to experience at the Magic Kingdom.

Fittingly, Walt Disney's name is the first and last one you'll see on Main Street, U.S.A., just as the Director of a movie is listed at both the opening and ending of the credits. Guests are greeted by a window at the Main Street Railroad Station which reads, "Walt Disney World Railroad Office - Keeping Dreams on Track - Walter E. Disney - Chief Engineer". A second window for Walt can be found at the far end of Main Street, U.S.A. on the second floor of the Plaza Ice Cream Parlor, facing Cinderella Castle.

Walt's brother, Roy O. Disney, was very instrumental in the creation of Walt Disney World and has a credit listed in a window above the Main Street Bakery. Having your name included on a Main Street, U.S.A. window is considered one of the highest honors of working at The Walt Disney Company.

www.Disney-Secrets.com

A WDW Guided Tours Tip:

To enjoy the shows on the Cinderella Castle forecourt stage, arrive 10 - 15 minutes prior to showtime to get a fantastic viewing spot. These shows get thousands of guests, but most don't show up until they hear the music begin playing.

Courtesy of WDWGuidedTours.com

CHAPTER THREE

SECRETS OF TOWN SQUARE

"You can design and create and build the most wonderful place in the world, but it takes people to make the dream a reality.

- Walt Disney

A TRIBUTE TO WALT'S BROTHER

As you enter Town Square, take a moment to find the life-size bronze statue of Roy O. Disney and Minnie Mouse sitting on a park bench. It's a fitting tribute to Walt's brother, Roy O. Disney, and his tireless efforts to fulfill his brother's wishes to create Walt Disney World after Walt's passing in 1966.

Note: If you arrive shortly after the Magic Kingdom's opening, this area may be crowded with character greetings, so you may wish to visit it later in the day.

Nearby, you'll also find a bronze plaque which contains the text of Roy O. Disney's opening day remarks in 1971.

"Walt Disney World is a tribute to the philosophy and life of Walter Elias Disney . . . and to the talents, the dedication, and the loyalty of the entire Disney organization that made Walt Disney's dream come true. May Walt Disney World bring Joy and Inspiration and New Knowledge to all who come to this happy place . . . a Magic Kingdom where the young at heart of all ages can laugh and play and learn - together."

MAKE YOUR DAY SPECIAL

Happy Birthday!, Happy Anniversary! and Happy 1st Visit to the Magic Kingdom! If any one of these special occasions apply to your visit, or if you're newly married or on a family reunion, be sure to stop in at City Hall or one of the Vacation Planning Booths and ask for a button  that tells everyone of your special event. Cast Members will make a special effort to recognize you throughout your day in the park.

In Honor of Veterans

If you're a Veteran, then you're a special guest at the Magic Kingdom. Stop by Guest Relations in City Hall and inquire about participating in the daily Flag Retreat Ceremony in Town Square. Every evening, Disney officials escort a Veteran to the flagpole in the center of the square for an honorary lowering of the flag. The ceremony lasts about 15 minutes and is a patriotic event the entire family will enjoy. The ceremony typically begins at 5:00 p.m., though this time can vary with the time of year.

A Tribute to Opening Day

As you exit City Hall, notice the Fire Station next door, which houses Engine Company 71. More than just a random number, the Disney Imagineers chose 71 in honor of the year in which the Magic Kingdom opened, 1971.

A Patchwork of Respect

Step inside the Fire Station and you'll discover a collection of antique fire-fighting equipment, as well as countless fire station patches and other insignias from stations all across the country honoring the brave men and women who serve and protect us on a daily basis.

www.Disney-Secrets.com

LOOK GOOD FOR YOUR VISIT

Now journey next door to find the old-fashioned Harmony Barber Shop, established in 1886. The secret . . . it's a real barber shop, and you can actually get your hair cut in the Magic Kingdom! Skilled barbers will trim, style, color and coif your hair, topping it all off with colorful pixie dust to give you a styling or even festive look for a day in the park. A "My First Haircut" package, which is popular with young children, provides patrons with their very first hair cut, special Mickey Mouse ears and a certificate honoring the occasion. And if you're lucky, you may even be serenaded by the Dapper Dans barbershop quartet.

Although small, the Harmony Barber Shop performs between 350 and 400 services a week. Children's "First Haircuts" are the establishment's specialty. If you arrive at the park's opening, or shortly thereafter, plan on waiting in line.

YOUR FIRST HIDDEN MICKEY OF THE DAY

One of the first Hidden Mickey's you'll discover in the Magic Kingdom is right inside the left entrance portal. Make your way over to the Horse Barn and look inside to the left. There, you'll see a horse bridle hanging with a classic 3-circle Hidden Mickey on the front. If it's not there, then look for it being worn by one of the horses out in Town Square or on Main Street, U.S.A.

OSH POPHAM

At the main entrance to The Emporium you'll find two large windows, and at the base of each window you'll see *"Osh" Popham – Proprietor* written in gold lettering. This is a nod to Osh Popham, a character in Disney's 1963 film *Summer Magic.* In the film, Oscar-winning actor Burl Ives plays Osh Popham, who is a postmaster, carpenter, musician, and good Samaritan in the small town of Beulah,  Maine, as well as the owner and proprietor of the local hardware store.

OFFERING ONLY THE LATEST AND GREATEST

 Did you happen to catch the window in The Emporium that touts all of the latest goods and gadgets found inside? With electricity now arriving at the turn of the century, The Emporium offers only the "Latest and Greatest" goods, including...Electrical Lamps, Graphophone Talking Machines, Edison Kinetoscopes, Imported Glassware, and Ladies Wearing Apparel.

GAWRSH, THAT'S FUNNY!

Now stroll across the Town Square and find Goofy sitting on a bench in front of Tony's Town Square Restaurant. While others pass by or stop only briefly to get a picture, go ahead and sit down next to him. You may be surprised to find he thinks it's funny.

Note: Sometimes Goofy can be found elsewhere in the Town Square, as he likes to move around.

TONY'S TOWN SQUARE RESTAURANT

Tony's Town Square Restaurant? It's named for the Italian Chef who served the romantic spaghetti dinner to the two title characters, Lady and the Tramp, in the 1955 classic Disney animated film *Lady and the Tramp.*

LADY AND THE TRAMP IMPRINTS

Many Magic Kingdom secrets are hidden right out in the open, where they are walked over by countless guests without their ever noticing. The brown area in the streets of Liberty Square, the Bride's wedding ring at the Haunted Mansion, even the 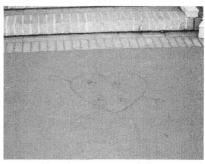 Utilidors. Here is another one you will not notice unless you look down. Make your way to the front of Tony's Town Square Restaurant and you'll find a large heart with paw prints belonging to Lady and the Tramp imprinted into the sidewalk. Note that this is sometimes obscured by strollers.

"WE CALL IT BELLA NOTTE"

 Step inside Tony's Town Square Restaurant and make your way to the back where you'll find Lady and the Tramp enjoying their spaghetti dinner together just outside the window in a romantic scene from their movie.

CALL WAITING

Now take a moment to step into The Chapeau, where you'll find an antique phone mounted on the wall. Most guests assume it's just a prop and walk right past it, but those who look closer find otherwise. Pick it up and listen in on a fun conversation between a mother and her daughter, Annie. Being the turn of the 20th century, Annie's mother is surprised that ham has now reached 11 cents per pound, and with things now so expensive, she advises Annie to marry a man who has $300 in savings and earns at least $8 per week.

Note: The phone seen here, which is a photo of the actual phone inside The Chapeau, is a second generation Western Electric Picture Frame Front Model 317 Wall Telephone.

HAPPY BIRTHDAY TO YOU!

If it's your birthday, then don't pass by this opportunity to make it really special. While in The Chapeau, find a *Mickey Mouse Ears Happy Birthday Hat*. Much more than the celebratory birthday button you can pick up for free at City Hall, it announces your special day with a colorful and festive hat that lets everyone know you're another year "funner".

Note: Other birthday hats are also available in the shop or by calling Merchandise Guest Services at 877-560-6477 or visit www.DisneyParks.com/store

HATS OFF TO JOHN A. DISNEY

As you visit the shops of Main Street, U.S.A., you may come across an "antique" hat box from Disney Hatters of New York City. This is a nod by the Imagineers to John A. Disney, who opened a hat shop at 196 Third Avenue in New York in

1885. According to the Disney Archives, Mr. Disney was not related to Walt, but if you needed a high-quality top hat for walking down Main Street, U.S.A. in style, then Mr. Disney's shop was the place to get it.

A TASTY SECRET

It's one thing to buy and enjoy a tasty treat in the Magic Kingdom, but it's another to actually see how they are made. Here's your chance!

You may need a little luck on your part, but next to the south entrance to the Main Street Confectionery is a window, and it is here that, if your timing is right, you can watch a Cast Member spin up some fresh cotton candy for you to enjoy as you stroll down Main Street, U.S.A., just as Walt intended. Next, step inside the shop and watch as candymakers create all kinds of tasty treats, from chocolate covered caramels and s'mores to Mickey Mouse shaped Rice Krispies treats, peanut brittle, brownies, fresh-baked cookies and so much more.

NO GUMMING UP THE WORKS

As you journey throughout the Magic Kingdom today, notice how you won't find bits of gum all over the sidewalk, under the benches, stuck to railings, or elsewhere. That's because gum isn't sold anywhere within Walt Disney World Resort. I guess you'll just have to settle for a Mickey Mouse Ice Cream Bar!

www.Disney-Secrets.com

CHAPTER FOUR

SECRETS OF
MAIN STREET, U.S.A.

*"Main Street, U.S.A. is America at the turn of the century –
the crossroads of an era. The gas lamps and the electric
lamp – the horse drawn car and auto car. Main Street is
everyone's hometown – the heart line of America."*

- Walt Disney

FORCED PERSPECTIVE

As you begin to "walk right down the middle of Main Street, U.S.A.", study the building facades for a classic Disney trick of the eye. Here the Imagineers have designed and built the buildings on Main Street, U.S.A. with an optical illusion called "Forced Perspective." Using this technique, they made the buildings appear taller than they actually are. The street level floors were built to full scale at 12 feet in height, while the  second story was built slightly smaller at 10 feet and the third story smaller still at 8 feet. In addition, the windows of the second and third stories were built both narrower and shorter than the windows below to further the illusion of height.

THE DAWN OF A NEW ERA

 As with Disneyland, the Magic Kingdom's Main Street, U.S.A. represents many things, one of which is the dawn of a new era and an exciting moment in history...the arrival of new technologies and the advent of electricity. Gas street lamps are being replaced with electric models, horse-drawn trolleys now share the road with motorized jitneys, and building facades are beginning to be adorned with bright new electric bulbs.

Perhaps one of the best examples the Disney Imagineers used in capturing this transition to electricity and the new age is reflected in the street lamps adorning Main Street, U.S.A. If you stop and look, you'll notice they all have a lamp similar to a gas flame. There was a time in America's history in which all street lamps were powered by gas, and every evening Lamplighters would make their way from lamp to lamp to light the flames as darkness approached. These lamps represent the "old" technology of gas flame, while the "new" technology of electricity is beginning to appear throughout Town Square, Main Street, U.S.A., and even The Hub. Combined, these old and new technologies work together as an interesting story element to tell of this fast-paced period of transition.

AMERICA'S FIRST STREET LAMP

On February 7, 1817, Baltimore, Maryland made history with the installation of the very first gas street lamp used in the United States. Standing at the corner of North Holliday and East Baltimore streets, it dutifully performed its task for 180 years before being replaced with a replica in 1997. Today, as the only working gas street lamp remaining in Baltimore, this single lamp stands on that corner as a monument to its important role in American history.

When designing Main Street, U.S.A., the Imagineers could have chosen any one of the hundreds of gas street lamp designs that were in use across the country during the turn of the 20th century. However, they instead chose a design with historical significance. The gas street lamps guests see lining Main Street, U.S.A. are *exact duplicates* of the historical lamp found in Baltimore, and as such each represents the very first gas street lamp used in America.

Note: When Baltimore began selling its surplus gas lamps in the 1950s, a number of them were bought by Imagineer Emile Kuri for installation at Disneyland, where they are in use today. While these are similar in design, they are not exact duplicates of the first gas lamp used in the United States, nor those installed on Walt Disney World's Main Street, U.S.A. in the Magic Kingdom.

HORSE AND BUGGY AND JITNEY

Main Street, U.S.A. represents an exciting time of change in turn-of-the-20th-century America, and another accurate representation of this are the colorful Main Street Vehicles transporting guests up and down the street.

In 1900, all modes of transportation on America's streets, including trolleys, buggies and carts, were pulled by horses, but beginning in 1905, the automobile began to make its appearance, and by 1915, only ten short years, horse pulled vehicles were largely a thing of the past. On Main Street, U.S.A., guests are immersed in this same transitional period in history as they are surrounded by both horse drawn *and* combustion powered vehicles transporting guests on their way to magic, adventure, and the future.

A FUN NEW PERSPECTIVE

It's so easy to dismiss the vehicles of Main Street, U.S.A. as only simple attractions that pale in comparison to some of the classics, such as Pirates of the Caribbean or Space Mountain, but they are actually a key to a whole new way to experience the magic.

If it's your very first visit to the Magic Kingdom, then you'll want to "stroll right down the middle of Main Street, U.S.A.", but if you've been many times, then do not walk past these attractions, but instead make it a point to hop aboard the Horse and Trolley, a Main Street Jitney or Fire Engine #71 while in Town Square and *ride down Main Street, U.S.A.* while enjoying the tremendous view as it unfolds all around you. It's an exciting new way to experience this area of the park as you ride through the hustle and bustle toward Cinderella Castle.

THE FLAGS OF
MAIN STREET, U.S.A.

As Walt created Main Street, U.S.A., he knew that even the smallest of details would not only enhance the story, but also help to make the magic real. One of the details he included can be found in the flags flying atop each of the buildings lining Main Street, U.S.A. It's difficult to notice, since they are usually flying in the breeze or draped closed when the wind is still, but each flag has 13 stripes, which is standard for an  American flag, but only 45 stars instead of 50. Why? Because Main Street, U.S.A. is set at a time that represents the turn of the 20th century, from a period of about 1890 to 1910. For much of this time, America had only 45 states, not today's total of 50, and as a result the flags you see above Main Street, U.S.A. display the proper and period-specific number of 45 stars arranged in the very same pattern as American flags flown in our country from July 4th, 1896 to July 3rd, 1908.

Keep an eye out, because you'll see this same attention to detail in flags found elsewhere in the Magic Kingdom, including Frontierland and Liberty Square.

ALONE ON MAIN STREET, U.S.A.

Have you ever wished you could have Main Street, U.S.A. all to yourself? Without all the crowds and with an unobstructed view of Cinderella Castle, perfect for taking pictures? With this next secret, you just might.

Disney offers an informative tour called Marceline to Magic Kingdom, which begins at 8:15 a.m. Book this tour on a morning in which The Magic Kingdom opens at 9:00 a.m. *and you'll be allowed into the park 45 minutes early. Arrive even earlier, and you may have time available to stroll up and down Main Street, U.S.A. while the tour assembles.* Be sure to have your camera ready, because this is the moment you've been waiting for! As one who has had the pleasure of photographing Main Street, U.S.A. and all of the park before it opened to any guests whatsoever, I can tell you that this is a surreal, yet very amazing experience.

You can book this tour by calling 407-939-8687. As an alternative, you may also book an early breakfast at Cinderella's Royal Table. This will also get you into The Magic Kingdom early, but you will not be able to move about, and it is much more expensive than the Marceline to Magic Kingdom tour.

WALT'S BOYHOOD TOWN

As with Disneyland, the Magic Kingdom's Main Street, U.S.A. is modeled after the town Walt Disney lived in as a young boy, Marceline, Missouri.

A WINDOW INTO HISTORY

You'll often hear that Walt designed the storefront windows of Main Street, U.S.A. to be low so that even small children could easily look inside and see their magical displays, but this is actually a "Magic Kingdom urban legend." Instead, the low window displays are another example of the Imagineers' attention to detail.

As indicated by the "Est. 1886" sign on the Harmony Barber Shop in Town Square, Main Street, U.S.A. represents turn-of-the-20th-century America. In this era, before the Internet, television and even radio, shop owners had to rely upon their window displays as their primary means of advertising. As a result, they typically built them as large as they could, often reaching nearly to the sidewalk, so as to show off as much merchandise as possible to passing customers.

SOUNDS LIKE DISNEY WHIMSY

Here's a fun secret that the Disney Imagineers created to capture the small town feel of Main Street, U.S.A. while adding another hidden story element with a whimsical touch. Like so many secrets, it's revealed only to those who pause and observe. As you journey up Main Street, U.S.A., take a right onto Center Street and look for the windows at the end of the street that read, "Singing Lessons" and "Music and Dance Lessons." Listen carefully below the windows and you'll eavesdrop on some rather comical encounters!

HISTORICAL CRYSTAL ARTS

More than just a destination at which to buy unique handcrafted Magic Kingdom works of art and souvenirs, Main Street, U.S.A.'s Crystal Arts shop has a history that reaches back to the earliest days of Disneyland.

While visiting the Spain pavilion at the 1964 / 1965 New York World's Fair, Walt Disney had the opportunity to meet Tomas and Alfonso Arribas, who were creating captivating works of art in an exhibit showcasing their 100 year-old glass blowing and crystal cutting business. Walt was so impressed by their mastery of the art that he invited them to open a shop at Disneyland, and in 1967 they began crafting Disney characters and collectibles in a small shop inside Sleeping Beauty Castle. Today, they operate Crystal Arts locations in 19 Disney parks around the world. Step inside to watch them handcraft figurines using a torch at the front of the shop, or make your way to the back where a skilled glassblower operates two large furnaces to hand forge beautiful pieces made of colorful glass. BTW, the Mickey Mouse vase seen here is one of their best sellers.

LEGENDARY GUEST SERVICE

Disney's commitment to the guest experience is legendary. As you visit the shops on Main Street, U.S.A., be aware that should you purchase anything and it breaks during your visit, Disney will replace it free of charge. This includes broken souvenirs, lost balloons, even dropped trays of food, ice cream, churros, etc.

Tip: Here's a tip just for parents. If your child really wants a Mickey or Minnie Mouse balloon to make their day at the Magic Kingdom extra special, you'll discover they're sometimes hard to find. Head over to Main Street, U.S.A. and there's a good chance you'll find a balloon vendor near Center Street, especially early in the day.

www.Disney-Secrets.com

ONE OF WALT'S
FAVORITE TREATS

As you make your way down Main Street, U.S.A., you are surrounded by tributes to Cast Members, notable Imagineers and even Walt Disney himself.

At the far end of Main Street, U.S.A. sits the Plaza Ice Cream Parlor, where guests will find two tributes to Walt. The first is the parlor itself. Ice cream was one of Walt's favorite treats, so he made sure to include the Gibson Girl Ice Cream Parlor in Disneyland so his guests could also enjoy this tasty treat. Here, in the Magic Kingdom, the Imagineers have paid tribute to Walt and his vision by including the Plaza Ice Cream Parlor when they designed the park. The second tribute is a large window dedicated to "Walter E. Disney", which you will find on the balcony of the Plaza Ice Cream Parlor, behind a railing. Fittingly, it faces Cinderella Castle.

THE SMOKE TREE RANCH

Now make your way to the "Partners" statue of Walt and Mickey Mouse and closely study Walt's tie. There you will find a symbol made up of three letters, "STR", which refer to the Smoke Tree Ranch in Palm Springs, California. Walt and his wife, Lillian, greatly enjoyed visiting the ranch whenever Walt could take a break from his many different projects. In fact, they enjoyed it so much that they chose to build a second home there.

However, Walt sold the home to help fund the construction of Disneyland, but this turned out to be a wise decision, as Disneyland proved to be such a success that he later built a new home at Smoke Tree Ranch, one that was even larger than the original.

WATCHING "HAPPILY EVER AFTER" FROM CALIFORNIA

At the end of the day, many guests choose to watch the *Happily Ever After* fireworks spectacular from Main Street, U.S.A. This is a great spot to see perhaps the best show in the park, as an abundance of fireworks explode in the air directly above Cinderella Castle as the castle takes center stage with colorful, lively, and dramatic scenes from your favorite Disney films projected across its facade, all set to classic Disney songs. However, unknown to many, you can also see the fireworks from The California Grill, found at the top of the Contemporary Resort just outside the park. At the time of the show, the restaurant dims the lights and plays the same music heard at the Magic Kingdom. It's a unique perspective on this magical performance!

Tip: Guests will also find many other locations throughout the Magic Kingdom offer a fun new perspective on *Happily Ever After*, including Fantasyland, Splash Mountain and even Disney's Polynesian Resort, though directly in front of Cinderella Castle gives you the best seat in the house.

THE WINDOWS OF
MAIN STREET, U.S.A.

As you walk down Main Street, U.S.A., you'll notice many different windows on the second and third stories of the buildings lining the street which honor Disney Legends, Imagineers, and others who have made a significant contribution to the Walt Disney Company. Here are just a few of these notable windows.

**Broggie's Buggies
Hand Made Wagons
Surreys Sleighs
Roger Broggie Wheelwright**

Near the entrance to the Horse Barn is a window honoring **Roger E. Broggie**, a Disney Legend who started his Disney career as a precision machinist in 1939 and later went on to play a major role in the development of Disneyland, eventually becoming the Vice President of WED Enterprises.

In addition, he is credited with introducing Walt Disney to the world of small-gauge railroading, going over to Walt's home on Carolwood Drive to help him build and install the Carolwood Pacific Railroad in Walt's backyard.

Iwerks – Iwerks
Stereoscopic Cameras
Ub Iwerks
Don Iwerks
"No Two Exactly Alike"

Ub Iwerks was there when Walt started it all, and he played a notable and significant role in developing the foundation for all of what the Walt Disney Company has become today.

Walt first met Ub Iwerks in 1919 when the two of them worked for the Pesmen-Rubin Commercial Art Studio in downtown Kansas City. In time, through a number of starts, stops, and detours, Ub ended up working for Walt at the Disney Brothers Cartoon Studio in Hollywood, California. It was there that Ub was credited with giving life to the image of Mickey Mouse, at Walt's direction, and shortly thereafter had animated Mickey Mouse's first cartoon, *Plane Crazy*, as well as his first sound cartoon, *Steamboat Willie.*

The reference to "No Two Exactly Alike" is no doubt a nod to Ub's animation skills, drawing literally tens and tens of thousands of animations during his career, each slightly different than the other so as to convey motion. Note that Don Iwerks is Ub's son, a former Disney executive and Co-Founder of Iwerks Entertainment.

www.Disney-Secrets.com

Seven Summits Expeditions
Frank G. Wells
President
"For those who want to do it all"

High above the Crystal Arts gift shop is a window in honor of **Frank Wells**, who was the former President and Chief Operating Officer of The Walt Disney Company and is credited with generating unprecedented growth in nearly all areas of the company during his tenure, from 1984 to 1994, from films and international expansion to the theme parks and Disney merchandise.

Of note is the lofty placement of this window, as well as the reference to "Seven Summits Expeditions". In 1983, Frank Wells set out to achieve the goal of ascending the highest peak on each of the seven continents within one year. He reached them all before being turned back near the top of Mt. Everest.

A WDW Guided Tours Tip:

For a great spot to enjoy the parade, head over to near the Harmony Barber Shop, in Town Square. Most guests don't know that the parade ends near here, and there are usually spots still open very close to the starting time for the parade.

Courtesy of WDWGuidedTours.com

CHAPTER FIVE

SECRETS OF ADVENTURELAND

"Here is adventure. Here is romance. Here is mystery. Tropical rivers – silently flowing into the unknown. The unbelievable splendor of exotic flowers...the eerie sound of the jungle...with eyes that are watching. This is Adventureland."

- Walt Disney

Bwana Bob's

You may have noticed on your way into Adventureland a merchandise kiosk called Bwana Bob's. Adorned with a thatched roof, tribal masks and bamboo, this kiosk offering hats, sunglasses, souvenirs and more is an homage to Bob Hope, who, as a fan of Walt Disney and his work, was the star of the 1963 film, *Call Me Bwana*, and a guest on the NBC TV special that opened Walt Disney World in October of 1971.

Did You Have To Bring the Snake?!

While dining at the Jungle Navigation Co. LTD Skipper Canteen, you'll notice up on a shelf marked "Lost and Found" a metal toolbox with the name of *J. Lindsey* written on the lid, along with a large sticker on its side which reads WARNING – MAY CONTAIN LIVE SNAKE. When setting out on an adventure, Indiana Jones would often travel to...or sometimes narrowly escape from...his destination by flying, and the pilot of his aircraft was always Jock Lindsey. Indy and Jock were good friends, but, much to Indy's dismay, Jock had the habit of always bringing along with him his pet boa constrictor, Reggie.

THE MAGIC CARPETS OF ALADDIN

One of the fun secrets about the Magic Kingdom is how Disney Imagineers often whimsically extend the story of an attraction beyond the attraction itself, and The Magic Carpets of Aladdin is a perfect example of this.

As you approach the attraction, find the large golden camel near the attraction's sign. Camels, such as those in Aladdin's world, are known to spit, and this one is no exception. Here the Imagineers have arranged for this camel to periodically "spit" water at passing guests, often with surprising accuracy!

A CHARMING HIDDEN MICKEY

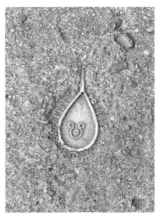

Upon leaving The Magic Carpets of Aladdin, make your way over to the entrance of the Agrabah Bazaar to find a small Hidden Mickey that thousands of guests walk over each and every day without ever realizing it is there.

Near the entrance to the Agrabah Bazaar is a pole holding up a fabric awning. Not far from the base of the pole is a group of white stones set into the pavement, and not far from these stones is a metal charm that holds a Hidden Mickey, no doubt dropped by a peddler selling his wares. *Photo courtesy of WDWGuidedTours.com*

www.Disney-Secrets.com

MIND THE EURYPELMA

There are many dangers awaiting you on the Jungle Cruise. Lions, tigers, bull elephants, hippos wiggling their ears... they're all lurking deep in the jungle, but one creature always gets the first opportunity to "interact" with unsuspecting guests. While winding your way through the queue, look for the small wooden cage labeled Tarantula (Eurypelma). It may appear at rest, but it's secretly waiting for you to get closer...closer...closer...

I DO KNOW THAT THE HIDDEN MICKEY IS TRUE

While braving the rivers of the Jungle Cruise, you'll come across the back half of a silver plane fuselage. Slowly being consumed by the dense jungle, it sits on a riverbank, no doubt with a harrowing tale to tell. The most common rumor you hear about it is that it's the back half of the plane that used to appear in *The Great Movie Ride* attraction at Disney's Hollywood Studios as a backdrop for Humphrey Bogart and Ingrid Bergman's famous scene in Casablanca, with some also believing that it's from the actual plane used in the film. That would then mean that this section of fuselage is the back half of a Lockheed Electra. However, while it shares some of the same characteristics as that plane, none of the designs of that aircraft ever had round windows, so this casts some serious doubt on those rumors. Another story you will hear is that it is part of the company plane that Walt Disney and his executives used to scout property while searching for a site upon which to build Walt Disney World Resort. That story is untrue, since that plane still exists and is intact. While there is a mystery surrounding

this plane, one thing is for certain, and that is the classic 3-circle Hidden Mickey riveted into its side. Look for it between the two windows, just above the foliage.

THE ORIGINAL JUNGLE CRUISE

So as to give all of the plants as much time as possible to grow and cover the Jungle Cruise landscape prior to Disneyland's opening in July of 1955, Walt made sure it was one of the first attractions created for his new park. Originally, he wanted the Jungle Cruise to be an authentic experience, complete with real animals. However, upon further reflection, Walt and his team realized that not only would wild animals be unpredictable in their behavior, but they tend to sleep during the day, which means guests on the attraction would probably not be able to see them as Walt intended. The fix?...Disney Imagineers used hydraulics to give motion to realistic looking animal figures, thus being able to control the "animals'" and have them appear active all throughout the day, every day.

A Tribute to Marc Davis

Hidden throughout Walt Disney World and Disneyland Resort are tributes to many Cast Members and Disney Imagineers who played a very important role in not only developing the theme parks, but The Walt Disney Company, as well. Many of these tributes are hidden in different attractions. For example, in the treasure room of the Pirates of the Caribbean, Disney Imagineers have placed a coat of arms with the name "Marco Daviso." It is a tribute to Marc Davis, one of Disney's "Nine Old Men" and the man responsible for animating many of Disney's well known characters, including Tinker Bell, Cruella De Vil and Cinderella. In addition, he was responsible for the story and character development of many classic Disney attractions, including the Haunted Mansion, "it's a small world", The Jungle Cruise and, of course, Pirates of the Caribbean.

Check the Checkmate, Mate

As you enter the Pirates of the Caribbean attraction, take the right queue line instead of the left and stop to peer into the dungeon windows on the right, shortly after you pass the turnstiles. There you will discover two chess-playing skeletons below. The rumor is  their match is deadlocked in a tie, which makes for a great story, but if you're a student of the game, you may think otherwise.

Note: Periodically, the pawns on the board are moved.

PLEASE WATCH YOUR STEP ...AND YOUR PEG!

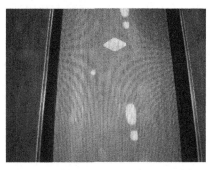

You may have noticed as you exit many attractions throughout the park and step upon a moving walkway that footprints are painted on the walkway surface to indicate the direction in which guests should proceed. Take note of the "foot prints" the Imagineers have placed on the moving walkway as you exit the Pirates of the Caribbean attraction. Those are the markings belonging to a peg-legged pirate!

THE DOLE WHIP

Turkey legs, Mickey Mouse ice cream bars and even churros are some of the iconic treats at Walt Disney World, yet the popular Dole Whip holds a special place in many guests' hearts, and a trip to the Magic Kingdom wouldn't be complete without one. In fact, the Dole Whip is such a treasured tradition it even has its own collectible pin!

Admittedly, this is a well-known "secret", but if you're like the many who have walked right past the Dole Whip counter while wondering why there is a long line, then you need to stop and find out why. They're lining up for the delicious Dole Whip, a classic Magic Kingdom treat you'll remember long after your vacation ends. Look for the Dole Whip next to the Enchanted Tiki-Room, opposite The Magic Carpets of Aladdin.

Tip: You can also get a Dole Whip at the Pineapple Lanai at Disney's Polynesian Resort.

NOW A ROUGH ADVENTURE

Now pause for a moment and notice one of the subtle changes that has occurred since you left Main Street, U.S.A. No longer are there streets defined by level brick walkways and crisp curbs, but instead you find rough uneven paths disappearing into the undergrowth, and instead of the finely pruned trees and shrubs of the Hub, the jungle is dense and overgrown...perfect for an adventure.

A WDW Guided Tours Tip:

Head to Adventureland first thing in the morning, as it is the quietest land in the park right after opening. If you start with Jungle Cruise followed by Pirates of the Caribbean, you can usually enjoy all five Adventureland attractions in under 90 minutes.

Courtesy of WDWGuidedTours.com

www.Disney-Secrets.com

CHAPTER SIX

SECRETS OF FRONTIERLAND

"Here we experience the story of our country's past...the colorful drama of Frontier America in the exciting days of the covered wagon and the stagecoach...the advent of the railroad...and the romantic riverboat. Frontierland is a tribute to the faith, courage, and ingenuity of the pioneers who blazed the trails across America."

- Walt Disney

Addressing This Secret

The stage that is the Magic Kingdom is filled with countless small details, most of which are easily overlooked, yet when discovered reveal another interesting element of the story. For example, take a look at the address numbers found throughout Frontierland. Note how they are not in chronological order, but instead are designed to represent the year in which the building was constructed. The Hall of Presidents was built in 1787, while the Town Hall of Frontierland was built in 1867 and the General Store in 1876.

Only 35 Stars in Frontierland

Even the flags displayed in Frontierland represent the era in which they are flying. Take note of the flag hung from the lookout tower next to the main walkway in Frontierland, and you'll see that it displays 13 stripes with only 35 stars, thus representing a brief two year period, from July 4th, 1863 through July 3rd, 1865, when America had only 35 states.

COUNTRY BEAR JAMBOREE

While you're waiting to see Big Al and the rest of the Country Bear Jamboree perform, take note of the claw marks they've left in the floor of the waiting area!

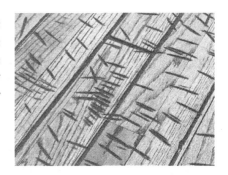

I'M WITH THE BAND

Unknown to most guests is that the lead character in the *Country Bear Jamboree*, Big Al, was based upon a real person, Imagineer Al Bertino. According to his daughter, Al was so animated and gregarious that his fellow Imagineers decided to make him into the character of Big Al, and if you look closely at the Animatronic character in the band, you'll see he looks exactly like Al Bertino.

A.C. DIETZ COMPANY LANTERNS

If you mosey over to the General Store in Frontierland, you'll see on an exterior wall a small sign that reads, *A.C. Dietz Co. - Importer of Coal Oil Lamps - Hardware - Harness - A Complete Line of Saddles.*

Typically, in a manner similar to the windows on Main

Street, U.S.A., a sign such as this pays homage to an individual who played an important role within The Walt Disney Company, such as a notable animator, an innovative Imagineer, or someone who helped build Walt Disney World Resort. However, in this case, this sign recognizes someone outside the world of Disney with an obscure but definite connection to Walt Disney and the early days of Disneyland!

In 1955, when Walt was building his brand new park, Disneyland, he bought all of the lanterns used in Frontierland from the R.E. Dietz Lantern Company. That appears to be a clear connection to this sign, but nobody named A.C. Dietz had ever worked for the company. However, the Founder, Robert E. Dietz, did have a cousin in San Francisco who owned and ran a General Store during the 1850s much like the one upon which this sign is affixed. Located at 224 Front Street, it provided all of the supplies the rugged forty-niners of the California Gold Rush needed to work their claims, including harnesses and saddles for their horses, bags of grain, wire, mining equipment and coal oil lanterns made by the Dietz Lantern Company. And the name of this cousin who owned the General Store... *Alfred Clinch Dietz*!

Now if you were to look closely at the lantern hanging on the wall by the A.C. Dietz sign, you would assume it was made by the Dietz Lantern Company, but instead it was manufactured by W.T. Kirkman Lanterns, Inc. Why isn't it a Dietz Lantern? Because the original Dietz lanterns Walt bought for Disneyland and the early days of Walt Disney World were manufactured using components made of tin. Unfortunately, those components wore out over time and the lanterns needed replacing. The Disney Imagineers turned to W.T. Kirkman

Lanterns to provide them with new galvanized steel models that do not rust but instead stand up better in today's weather...or that of the 1850s. (Or in this case, 1876, which ties in with the address of the Frontierland General Store.)

My thanks to Woody Kirkman of W.T. Kirkman Lanterns, Inc. for his generous contribution to this story.

UNCLE KEPPLE & SONS

Visit the General Store in Frontierland, and you're likely to see some bags of "Uncle Kepple & Sons" livestock feed. On the face of it, this is a simple nod to Walt Disney's grandfather, Kepple Disney. However, as with many of the Disney Imagineers' secrets, there's a bit more to this intriguing story.

Based upon the nearby sign referring to A.C. Dietz, who ran a General Store like the one in Frontierland in San Francisco during the California Gold Rush, one could assume these bags acknowledge Kepple Disney's setting out in 1877 with his sons Robert and Elias (Walt's father) on a journey to California to search for gold. They never made it, however, as Kepple instead decided to stop and settle in Kansas, where he purchased over 300 acres in Ellis County from the Union Pacific Railroad and established a farm. *Photo courtesy of WDWGuidedTours.com*

FRONTIERLAND
SHOOTIN' ARCADE

They don't know it, but many guests walk past The Frontierland Shootin' Arcade and miss out on an opportunity to practice their wild west shooting technique for free. Be one of the first guests of the day to stop by and test your shooting prowess and you may be rewarded with a few free rounds, as each morning random rifles at the Frontierland Shootin' Arcade are "pre-loaded" with rounds on the house.

Note: The Frontierland Shootin' Arcade is a classic attraction that dates back to opening day at Disneyland, and it is one of the few attractions in the park that requires an extra fee.

A HIDDEN MICKEY SET IN STONE

Tens of thousands of guests walk by everyday without ever noticing it, but hidden from view on the bridge to the lower section of Splash Mountain is a classic Hidden Mickey made of three stones. To find it, look on the bridge support that faces toward Tom Sawyer Island.

HARPER'S MILL

Situated on the south shore of Tom Sawyer Island is the deserted Harper's Mill, an old grist mill filled with large spinning wooden gears that used to grind grain into flour. Like the windows on Main Street, U.S.A., the mill is also a tribute to Harper Goff, a Disney Legend, Imagineer, artist and production designer who was involved in the design and production of classic Disney films, as well as such attractions as Main Street, U.S.A., the Jungle Cruise at Disneyland and World Showcase at Epcot.

It is rumored that the creaks and groans of the mill wheel plays the song "Down by the Old Mill Stream". However, I've listened and didn't find this to be the case. Others swear by it, though. That said, make sure you find your way onto Tom Sawyer Island and peer inside Harper's Mill to see the spinning gears. It's an attention to detail many guests miss and it really adds to the Tom Sawyer Island story.

"UNLESS SOME NO GOOD DONE SCARED EM"

As you enter Harper's Mill, you'll pass a sign posted by Tom Sawyer that reads...

This here deserted grist mill was named after my frien Joe Harpers old man Ifn you chooze to go inside please don't scare the birds what will you find there unless some no good done scared em before you did.

What Tom is referring to are a couple of birds that represent a nod to Walt Disney's 1937 academy award-winning animated short film *The Old Mill*. In this film, an old windmill is home to an assortment of small animals, including some bats, mice, a couple of doves, a wise owl in the rafters above, and a pair of blue birds tending their nest of eggs, which they have built in the gap of an old cog wheel. Step inside Harper's Mill and look carefully at the large spinning gears to find a small bluebird going around and around as she sits atop a straw nest she's built between two large gear teeth. Now look up and you'll find, perched in the rafters, an owl looking down at you with the same level of disdain as the owl in *The Old Mill*.

TOM PICKED UP ALL OF THE BRUSHES

Here's a classic Walt Disney World Secret that is no more. It used to be that a special prize awaited those guests who found this next secret...a FastPass to Splash Mountain or Big Thunder Mountain Railroad.

At the beginning of each day, cast members would hide a few paint brushes throughout Tom Sawyer Island. Each would be covered in whitewash and read...

"Tom Sawyer Paintbrush - In order to complete his chores, Tom needs to whitewash Aunt Polly's fence. Unfortunately, in his play time, he managed to lose the brushes all over the island. If you happen to pick up this brush, please return it to the raft driver. Remember only one brush per family. Thank you."

Lucky guests who found a paintbrush could return it to the raft driver and receive a FastPass for Splash Mountain or Big Thunder Mountain, which was valid all day long. However, both Tom and Huck returned to Hannibal a while ago and picked up all of the brushes, so they are no longer hidden for guests to find. Perhaps one day Tom will lose them again.

A LITERARY FENCE

Give it a casual glance and you'll think it's just a work in progress, an unpainted fence waiting for someone to come along and finish the job. However, if you look again and pay attention to the names and the color, you'll see it's the famed whitewashed fence from  the classic Mark Twain tale, *The Adventures of Tom Sawyer.*

AUNT POLLY'S ROCKING CHAIRS

Finding a place to sit away from the busy pace of the Magic Kingdom is an attraction in itself. Having that place be two large rocking chairs is all the better. Just down from the whitewashed fence, near Aunt Polly's, you'll find two comfortable rocking chairs waiting for you. Take a seat and enjoy a great view of the Haunted Mansion, as well as an up close view of the Liberty Square Riverboat as it passes on its way to its dock.

PAPPY'S PIER

 Head over to the other side of Tom Sawyer Island, opposite Big Thunder Mountain Railroad, and you'll find Pappy's Pier, a quiet out-of-the-way dock with a couple of wooden rocking chairs offering a nice respite and an

entertaining view of Big Thunder Mountain Railroad and the passing Liberty Square Riverboat.

A FAMILIAR BUCKBOARD

A trip from Big Thunder Mountain over to Tom Sawyer Island takes you back in time to another place, but it also takes you right back to Big Thunder Mountain! While standing on the loading dock on the island, look up in the rafters and you'll find a hidden miniature Clarkdale Dry Goods buckboard, which is an exact duplicate of the full-sized Clarkdale Dry Goods buckboard found in the queue over at Big Thunder Mountain.

TOM SAWYER ISLAND TRIBUTES

Along with the Clarkdale Dry Goods buckboard, you'll also find a toolbox, washboard, beehive, and other items adorned with large initials, as well as a wooden case for *Professor Barry K's Elixir*. All of these are tributes to long time Disney Imagineers who have made notable contributions to the park. In the case of Professor Barry K., this is actually a tribute to Imagineer Barry K. Snyder, who told me that the wooden case was graciously made by a colleague of his in WDW Displays as an honor for his 40-year career with Disney and in the entertainment industry.

THE QUEUE OF
BIG THUNDER MOUNTAIN

In addition to all of the antique mining equipment that the Imagineers sourced from throughout the old west and brought in specifically for this attraction, the queue of Big Thunder Mountain is chock full of secret story elements. References to Imagineers, Disney movies, mining lore, and more await those who keep their eyes open. The following are just a few you'll find while waiting to ride "The Wildest Ride in the Wilderness!"

A TRIBUTE TO
TONY WAYNE BAXTER

Hidden throughout Big Thunder Mountain Railroad at the Magic Kingdom, and every park where this attraction exists, is a clever tribute to the Disney Imagineer credited with its creation. Located on the Builders Plates of each locomotive, as well as on signs  and old equipment, is a logo that includes the initials "BTM". On first glance, this is clearly a reference to "Big Thunder Mountain". However, if you study the "M", you'll see it looks more like an inverted "W", which it is. Pat Burke, the Disney Imagineer who acquired all of the antique mining equipment placed throughout the attraction from the old west, as well as gave the attraction its "rusty" appearance, purposely created this logo with the "W" upside down, so as to provide a cleverly hidden homage to the attraction's creator, Tony Wayne Baxter.

BARNABAS T. BULLION

As you make your way through the queue for Big Thunder Mountain Railroad, you can't help but notice a large oil painting of Barnabas T. Bullion, the Founder and President of the Big Thunder Mining Company. According to the Disney Imagineers...

This longtime mining magnate comes from a powerful East Coast family and considers gold to be his very birthright by virtue of his oddly appropriate name; in fact, he considers the ultimate gold strike to be his destiny. And that is why he is having so much trouble with Big Thunder Mountain. According to superstitious locals, Big Thunder Mountain is very protective of the gold it holds within, and the unfortunate soul who attempts to mine its riches is destined to fail. And so far, that prophecy is coming to pass. The mine has been plagued by mysterious forces and natural disasters ever since. And yet the Big Thunder Mining Company is still in operation. In fact, Bullion is discovering new veins of gold and digging new shafts every day, offering a closer look at the Big Thunder mining operation than ever before. But a word to the wise for anyone attempting to visit the mountain: watch out for runaway trains.

If you're thinking Mr. Bullion has a striking resemblance to Tony Baxter, you're right, he does. In fact, nobody has ever seen Mr. Baxter and Mr. Bullion together at the same time!

A Fast Fuse on a Quick Wit

In an example of the Imagineers' sense of humor, take note of the name on the open cases of dynamite found throughout the mine. If it eludes you, then just sound it out. Also notice that not only is the case in the accompanying photo open, but the fuses are exposed and ready to light!

Note the Musical Detail

That music you hear while waiting in the queue? According to Disney, it was all recorded using instruments that were popular during the 1880s, including a fiddle, harmonica, piano, and of course, the banjo.

An Apple Dumpling Secret

Making your way along the queue, you'll find a number of references to Disney's 1975 film, the *Apple Dumpling Gang*, in which Theodore Ogelvie (Don Knotts) and Amos Tucker (Tim Conway) are a couple of harmless and inept bumbling thieves in the town of Quake City, California, in 1879. No doubt a few scenes from the movie provided some inspiration for Big Thunder Mountain, especially the depiction of the cave-in of the Commodore Mine.

As you make your way along the queue, you'll spot a small poster from the T.W. Bullion mine in Nevada, (Tony Wayne Bullion) which warns you to be on the lookout for Theodore and Amos, who *"Fouled up our whole operation and took off with ten pounds of lead. Complete incompetents."*

THE BUTTERFLY STAGE LINE

That poster you spotted for the Butterfly Stage Line offers up a number of secret references, including a few for *The Apple Dumpling Gang*, three for Big Thunder Mountain Railroad attractions around the world, and even one for Walt Disney himself.

The Butterfly Stage Line, Colonel T.R. Clydesdale, and Quake City were story elements of *The Apple Dumpling Gang* movie, while Thunder Mesa, Tumbleweed, and Rainbow Ridge can be found at Big Thunder Mountain attractions in Paris, the Magic Kingdom, and Disneyland respectively, and the Carolwood-Pacific Railroad Company was the name of Walt Disney's personal railroad in the backyard of his home in the Holmby Hills neighborhood of Los Angeles, California.

SOMETHING IS MISSING

 In the days of old, miners would bring canaries in birdcages down into the mines with them as a rudimentary warning system. If any of the canaries stopped singing and died, then that indicated that there wasn't enough oxygen in the mine shaft, and all the miners should leave as quickly as possible, lest they meet the same fate as the canary. As you wait in the queue, take note of the bird cages hanging from the rafters overhead. Did you notice how they are all empty? This is not a good sign!

YOUR VERY OWN
CANARY IN A GOLD MINE

There is (mostly) good news about the missing canaries, however. Some can be found within the Autocanary, an air quality analyzer patented in 1865. While making your way through the queue, you'll pass a number of antique  Autocanary machines, each with a silver handle. Give the handle a turn, and you will be treated to an animation showing a live canary, provided your canary hasn't already expired!

WATCH FOR ANOTHER
CRITTER AT THE GOLD MINE

You may have noticed another critter waiting with you in the Big Thunder Mountain Railroad queue. Take a look while passing the small waterfall outside, in the early part of the queue, for a small frog or two. These aren't Animatronics, but instead are  real, live "Animal-tronics", who have taken up residence on Big Thunder Mountain. BTW, please don't bother the frogs.

TUMBLEWEED CABINET & CASKET CO.

Did you happen to catch the name of the business operating at the mine? Painted on the side of a coffin...which is appropriately placed atop the explosives shed...it reads *Tumbleweed Cabinet & Casket Co. - Furniture, Upholstery, & Embalming.* This is truly the wild west, indeed!

WHERE YOU SIT MAKES A DIFFERENCE

Ask someone in the know, and they will tell you that where you sit on some attraction vehicles makes all the difference in the world. Want to make your ride on Big Thunder Mountain even more exciting? Then remember to ask a Cast Member when you

reach the end of the queue line if you may sit in the back car of the mine train where the "wildest ride in the wilderness" is even wilder!

www.Disney-Secrets.com

THE FUSING CAGE

As you make your way through the queue of Big Thunder Mountain Railroad, you'll notice the door to the "Fusing Cage" is adorned with the names of notable Disney Imagineers who contributed to the development of the attraction. Here's a short bio for each...

Little Big Gibson – Blaine Gibson

In addition to providing animation for early Disney classic films, including Fantasia, Peter Pan and Sleeping Beauty, Blaine Gibson created hundreds of accurately detailed sculptures for such attractions as Great Moments with Mr. Lincoln, the Haunted Mansion, Pirates of the Caribbean and more. Perhaps his most famous work is of the bronze statue "Partners", which depicts Walt and Mickey standing hand in hand and can be found in the hub of Disney theme parks around the world.

Jolley the Kid – Bob Jolley

As Field Art Director, Bob Jolley used his Imagineering talents to combine Big Thunder Mountain Railroad's shiny new technology with its authentic mining past. Recognized as an expert in show finishes and skilled in the craft of aging story elements, he blended the new and old together to give the entire attraction the rustic historic look we see today.

Buckaroo Burke – Pat Burke

Pat Burke was the WDI Imagineer responsible for designing many of the attractions found throughout Disney theme parks worldwide, including four Big Thunder Mountains, four Indiana Jones, three Jungle Cruises and the original Splash Mountain. It is commonly known among guests that the authentic mining equipment found throughout these different attractions came from many different locations across the United States, and Pat Burke was the man who was responsible for discovering it all and bringing it to the parks.

Calamity Clem – Clem Hall

Clem Hall was a concept artist responsible for creating conceptual artwork for numerous Disneyland and Walt Disney World attractions, including Big Thunder Mountain Railroad.

Skittish Skip – Skip Lange

Skip Lange of Walt Disney Imagineering was responsible for designing the unique mountain landscape of Disneyland's Big Thunder Mountain Railroad, fashioning the look after the "hoodoos" found in Bryce Canyon National Park in Utah. He would go on to design the rockwork for every Big Thunder Mountain Railroad attraction found in Disney theme parks worldwide.

Wild Wolf Joerger – Fred Joerger

An important part of every attraction's development is the crafting of miniature 3-D models that represent how the attraction will look when finished. Fred Joerger, in addition to crafting models for early Disney movie sets and "most everything at Disneyland", was known as the "resident rock expert" because of his expertise in designing and crafting the large realistic stonework found throughout Disneyland and Walt Disney World, including the stonework found at the Jungle Cruise, Pirates of the Caribbean and Big Thunder Mountain Railroad.

Matchstick Marc - Marc Davis

This is a tribute to a Disney Legend and one of Disney's "Nine Old Men" of animation, Marc Davis. In addition to animating such classic Disney characters as Cinderella, Snow White, Tinker Bell, Cruella De Vil, Brer Rabbit, Bambi, Alice and others, Mr. Davis played an important role in the development of characters for many of your favorite attractions, including Pirates of the Caribbean, The Jungle Cruise, "it's a small world", The Country Bear Jamboree, the Haunted Mansion, The Enchanted Tiki Room and more.

This isn't the only homage to Marc Davis in the park, as guests will also find a tombstone at the Haunted Mansion which reads...

In Memory Of
Our Patriarch
Dear Departed
Grandpa
Marc

Mama Hutchinson - Helena Hutchinson

Helena Hutchinson practiced her craft in the Figure Finishing department at Walt Disney Imagineering, which was responsible for adorning the multitude of characters that appeared in the parks, be they birds, goats, buffaloes, tigers, skeletons or human figures, in everything from fur and paint to feathers and costumes. As an expert in working with fur, she finished the animals found throughout Big Thunder Mountain Railroad.

PROFESSOR CUMULUS ISOBAR

It passes by so quickly it's difficult to see, but just before you roar past the flooded town of Tumbleweed and dive into the Dave V. Jones Mine, look left and notice the wagon of Professor Cumulus Isobar, Rain Maker. Look quickly and you'll find the professor himself leaning out the front door while bailing out his wagon, all while his two donkeys stand to the side high and dry. His name, of course, is a nod to the Disney Imagineers' sometimes whimsical nature, as "Cumulus" is a type of cloud and "Isobar" is a measure of barometric pressure.

Tip: The scene of Professor Cumulus Isobar flies right by as you're riding BTMRR, but if you'd like to see a slower perspective of Big Thunder Mountain and get a shot similar to the one above, then hop aboard the Walt Disney World Railroad at the Main Street or Frontierland Stations and have your camera ready as the train travels past the scene.

A DIFFERENT TUNE AT NIGHT

Pass by the town of Tumbleweed at Big Thunder Mountain Railroad during the day and you'll notice that things are awfully quiet, as the miners are out working in the mines, but at night the town comes alive with lights, music, and a good deal of commotion.

GEAR UP TO QUICKLY
SPOT THIS HIDDEN MICKEY

Your wildest ride in the wilderness is wrapping up, but there is one more secret to spot as you return to the boarding area. On your right, laying amongst the gear wheels large and small dispersed on the ground, is a 3-circle Hidden Mickey made up of one very large gear wheel and two smaller ones. Be ready to spot it, as it goes by quickly.

A UNIQUE
BIG THUNDER MOUNTAIN PHOTO

All throughout the Magic Kingdom there are countless different perspectives of the park which everyone enjoys...the view of Cinderella Castle from Main Street, U.S.A., Splash Mountain from below the log flume drop, the pillaging pirates within Pirates of the Caribbean and perhaps a million other scenes visible everywhere guests turn, and while these perspectives of the story that is the Magic Kingdom are certainly a thrill, the real fun is discovering the rare new perspectives of the park which few guests ever see...Frontierland from *inside* the Liberty Square Riverboat wheelhouse, the town of Tumbleweed from the Walt Disney World Railroad, or perhaps even Main Street, U.S.A. from within the horse-pulled trolley.

Here's a new perspective of a favorite attraction that the Disney Imagineers have purposely hidden for you to find, yet

99% of guests miss. Even better, it gives you an opportunity to capture a dramatic photo of Big Thunder Mountain unlike any other!

As you approach Big Thunder Mountain Railroad, walk up and to the right toward the exit area. There you will find two exits to the attraction. Make your way to the top level exit and turn left at the fence where guests stop to watch the mine trains. Just before reaching the doorway, look for a large "crack" in the rocks on your right-hand side. If you stop here and look through the crack, you'll notice you can see the tracks from this hidden dead-on perspective. Now zoom in with your camera and take a picture just as the next train engine exits the mine and you'll have a fun photo unlike any other that gives the impression you were standing right on the tracks as the train raced toward you! Don't forget to shoot a video here, too. *Photos courtesy of WDWGuidedTours.com*

Splash Mountain

An FSU Weasel?

As you make your way through Splash Mountain, you'll begin to round a bend and spot Brer Fox holding Brer Rabbit inside a bee hive. Before reaching the bend, look up and spot a critter in the ceiling known by many as the "FSU Weasel," which periodically emerges and shouts something. Some believe it says, "FSU!", while others believe it's "If I's you!", a nod to the storyline which tells you at this point in the ride "I'd be turnin' around, if I was you.", for it is here you begin your climb to the 52 foot plunge into the briar patch!

All 'Board!...
The Zip-A-Dee Lady

This next secret is discovered only by those who make the effort to ride the Grand Circle Tour of the Walt Disney World Railroad, and of those who do see the secret, it usually takes them by surprise. Board the Walt Disney World Railroad and

keep watch to the right hand side as the train passes into Splash Mountain. Here, guests aboard the train are treated to a fun overhead perspective of other guests riding logs through Splash Mountain below as they make their way through the musical scene with the festive "Zip-A-Dee Lady" paddlewheeler.

ZIP-A-DEE HIDDEN MICKEY

The "Zip-A-Dee Lady" paddlewheeler scene also holds another classic Hidden Mickey, which, though easy to see, is a bit difficult to decipher. As you make your way through the scene in the hollowed-out Splash Mountain log, look up and to the right of  the paddlewheeler to find a large cloud. Study it carefully, and you'll find it's actually an image of Mickey Mouse lying on his back.

BRIAR RABBIT'S PLACE

 This next secret reveals something most guests never see, even though it is an integral part of the story of Splash Mountain. Br'er Rabbit set out from his home to find his "laughin' place", only to tangle with, and outwit, Br'er Bear and Br'er Fox before ultimately returning to the safety and comfort of his home and friends. Would you like to see his home to complete the story? Then step into the Briar Patch merchandise shop, in underneath the massive briars and roots poking through the ceiling, and look above in the back of the shop. There, you'll see his humble home, which he returned to after all of his wild adventures on Splash Mountain.

A HIDDEN REST

Parents wishing to give children a break can find the Laughin' Place play area in the shade under the train trestle by Splash Mountain. It can also be a great place for children to play while parents enjoy a ride or rest for a while.

IT'S RAILROAD MORSE

As you make your way through the queue to board the Walt Disney World Railroad, notice the door to the left at the top of the ramp. As with the New Orleans Train Station at Disneyland and the Main Street Railroad Station at the Magic Kingdom, the "Railroad Morse" code being tapped out from behind this door is a portion of Walt Disney's opening day speech at Disneyland in 1955.

A WDW Guided Tours Tip:

If someone in your party isn't riding Big Thunder Mountain, have them head up the hill near the exit of the ride for a great view. Although there is no "on-ride" photo for BTM, a "non-rider" can get a fantastic picture of the train as it races by.

Courtesy of WDWGuidedTours.com

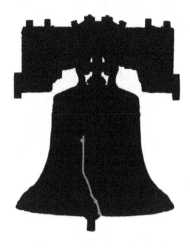

CHAPTER SEVEN

SECRETS OF
LIBERTY SQUARE

"Our heritage and ideals, our code and standards – the things we live by and teach our children – are preserved or diminished by how freely we exchange ideas and feelings."

- Walt Disney

LIBERTY SQUARE
MARCHES THROUGH TIME

The Magic Kingdom's Liberty Square was born from Walt's idea for an area at Disneyland called "Liberty Street." From the book *Disneyland In-Depth*...

Walt realized that he wanted this street to be a representation of Colonial America, an area of the park in which guests could acquire an understanding and appreciation of the Revolutionary War, our nation's Presidents, how enterprise helped shape our great country, and the dramatic struggles and events which won us all liberty and freedom.

Unfortunately, Walt's idea for Liberty Street never came to fruition, but the Imagineers never let go of the idea, and today it lives at Liberty Square.

While many guests simply walk through Liberty Square on their way to the Haunted Mansion or the attractions of Frontierland, you would be wise to stop and spend some time here, where you'll soon realize it slowly reveals a fascinating story, as well as many secrets.

The first secret reaches across a time span of over 100 years. Like the Norway Pavilion in Epcot, or Frontierland next door, all of the *architecture* and many of the *story elements* of

Liberty Square offer clues to the progression of time in Colonial America, from the late 1700s to the late 1800s, moving in a clockwise manner from the Haunted Mansion to the Hall of Presidents, over to the Ye Olde Christmas Shoppe and the Liberty Square Tavern before continuing west to Frontierland.

Beginning with the Haunted Mansion, we see a grand yet imposing (and haunted) structure influenced by the beautiful mansions and manors of the mid-1700s in what is now the Hudson River Valley National Heritage Area in New York, as well as the stately Harry Packer Mansion in Jim Thorpe, Pennsylvania.

Moving east, we now visit the Momento Mori merchandise shop, where its pre-Colonial (Georgian) architecture features a widow's walk surrounding a cupola up on the roof, which is perhaps a nod to the Haunted Mansion's Captain Culpepper Clyne, who "...braved the sea and all her wrath, but drowned on land while taking a bath."

Next is the Columbia Harbor House. Featuring multiple architectural styles serving to transition guests from Fantasyland, its facade facing Liberty Square features Dutch Colonial elements, along with some seafaring adornments.

To the right of the Columbia Harbor House, we begin to see buildings with a definitive Colonial or Georgian architecture, which was developed in England during the 17th century and featured as the prominent style of construction in the Pennsylvania area for about 100 years, from 1700 to 1800. Here, we see brick, fieldstone, or wood used to construct simple two to three story structures with rigid symmetry

reflected in the placement of key architectural elements, including paneled doors centered in the structure, and windows and chimneys placed such that they are balanced in appearance.

By now, we're seeing one of the first definitive story elements pointing to a specific date and year, for there in a second story window are two lamps arranged by Paul Revere to announce "One if by land, and two if by sea.", which occurred on April 18, 1775.

 The Revolutionary War of 1775 to 1783 has now begun, and this is reflected as you continue your walk clockwise. In a ground floor window is a musket, which was placed there by the homeowner to indicate that a civilian colonist living in the home is prepared to answer the call to fight. His goal is to be ready at a minute's notice, hence the name "Minutemen". The first Minutemen militia was formed in 1774.

Next up is the Hall of Presidents, bringing us to 1787, as indicated by the date appearing on its front gable. The largest of the structures found in Liberty Square, it introduces a more formal Federal style of architecture, which is a nod to the drafting of the United States Constitution, which occured in September of 1787.

As we move further east, we see more examples of Federal and Georgian architecture, as well as Dutch Colonial in the building behind the Ye Old Christmas Shoppe, but here you'll also notice that the buildings in this area all begin to share a similar feature...sagging window shutters.

In Colonial America, iron hardware was not readily available, since, due to the Iron Act of 1750, it was against the law for American colonies under British rule to produce iron goods, including shutter hinges. As a result, colonists were forced to buy hardware  from the British. Of course, these supplies were cut off during the Revolutionary War, so the colonists were now forced to use metal from any source they could find to build weapons and forge bullets. One of those sources was the shutter hinges. With the metal hinges given to the war effort, colonists replaced them with leather straps, but in time, the leather straps would stretch, causing the shutters to sag.

We're now at Sleepy Hollow Refreshments, which is a nod to the popular tale, *The Legend of Sleepy Hollow*, one of the earliest stories to emerge from America with enduring popularity. Originally published by Washington Irving in 1820, yet set in 1790 near Tarrytown, New York, it tells the haunting story of a headless horseman who terrorizes a local schoolmaster, Ichabod Crane. It is believed that Irving drew inspiration for the horseman from the tale of a Hessian soldier, who fought with the British and lost his head when he was decapitated by a cannonball in battle.

We've reached the apex, if you will, of our journey through Liberty Square, and that is the bridge leading into the square from the Hub. It is interesting to note that the original bridge built here, which existed from opening day in 1971 until it was replaced in 2000 and again in 2008, was designed by Disney Imagineer Herb Ryman to resemble the Old North Bridge, where the "shot heard around the world" occurred, thus beginning the American Revolutionary War, also known as the American War of Independence.

At this point, we've journeyed through the turn of the century and are now headed out west toward Frontierland. We're well into the 1800s now, as the Liberty Tree Tavern reflects Greek Revival architecture, a style that was very popular in the early 1820s, and one that was introduced to America in large part due to the efforts of Thomas Jefferson.

We'll wrap up our journey through Liberty Square by boarding the Liberty Square Riverboat sometime in the mid-1800s. Take note of the U.S. flags flying from the flag pole at the Liberty Square Riverboat dock, as well as aboard the Liberty Belle, and you'll see they fly with 31 stars, which all American flags displayed during a seven year period from July 4th, 1851 to July 3rd, 1858.

WATCH WHERE YOU STEP

This next secret is one that countless guests have walked right over without ever knowing it existed, though they may wish they did!

During America's colonial period, buildings lacked today's modern plumbing amenities, including toilets. As a result, people would pour their chamber pots containing waste matter out into the street gutters in front of their homes and businesses. Because there were no storm drains during this era, the waste would mix with rainwater and flow out into the unpaved streets. The brown "rivers" guests see winding their way down the streets throughout Liberty Square are a historically accurate nod to this unpleasant element of colonial life. *Photo courtesy of WDWGuidedTours.com*

YE OLDE CHRISTMAS SHOPPE

A stop inside the Ye Olde Christmas Shoppe reveals not one, but three different shops, each owned and decorated by a different colonial family; A woodcarver's family, a musician's family and a German family named Kepple, an homage to Walt Disney's grandfather, Kepple Disney.

A Priceless
Cheap Silhouette

While wandering through Liberty Square, you'll notice a cart offering a classic attraction imported from Disneyland...hand-cut silhouettes.

Why did the Disney Imagineers choose Liberty Square for the placement of this cart instead of Main Street, U.S.A.? Because the history of this unique art form fits perfectly with the timeline of Liberty Square.

In March of 1759, Monsieur Etienne de Silhouette was named as Controller-General of France, where he enacted measures of austerity in order to gain control of the country's finances. Unfortunately for him, this gave him the reputation of being a penny-pincher. About that same time, a new and inexpensive art form was beginning to be displayed in homes across the country by those who could not afford more expensive oil paintings or sculptures, and this new art form consisted of simply a dark image of an object displayed on a light background. Those who considered this to be an inexpensive form of art started referring to it as a "silhouette", implying it was as cheap as Monsieur Etienne de Silhouette. Through time the name took hold, and we still find it in use today, over 260 years later in Liberty Square.

THE LIBERTY TREE

Earlier, I mentioned Walt's idea for a new "Land" in Disneyland called "Liberty Street". Representing Colonial America, it would feature shops, restaurants and exhibits of the year 1775, and in the middle of its square would be a large oak tree adorned with 13 lanterns, each representing the original 13 colonies. Walt never built Liberty Street in Disneyland, but the Disney Imagineers brought the idea of The Liberty Tree to the Magic Kingdom's Liberty Square, complete with 13 lanterns representing the original 13 colonies.

Note: The Liberty Tree is a nearly 150 year-old live oak that was transplanted from another location at Walt Disney World. Its acorns are used by Disney landscaping engineers to grow saplings for other areas in the park.

IN CASE YOU MISSED IT

Located at the base of the Liberty Tree is a bronze plaque, placed when the park opened in 1971, which reads...

THE LIBERTY TREE

UNDER THE BOUGHS OF THE ORIGINAL LIBERTY TREE IN BOSTON IN 1765, PATRIOTS, CALLING THEMSELVES "THE SONS OF LIBERTY," GATHERED TO PROTEST THE IMPOSITION OF THE STAMP ACT. IN THE YEARS THAT FOLLOWED, ALMOST EVERY AMERICAN TOWN HAD A LIBERTY TREE – A LIVING SYMBOL OF THE AMERICAN FREEDOM OF SPEECH AND ASSEMBLY. OUR LIBERTY TREE IS A SOUTHERN LIVE OAK, QUERCUS VIRGINIANA, MORE THAN 100 YEARS OLD.

A NOD TO THE
ORIGINAL LIBERTY TREE

In the spring of 1765, England's Parliament approved The Stamp Act, which, among other things, would impose upon the colonists a tax on all printed materials, including newspapers, pamphlets, wills, deeds, even playing cards. Given this was well before the  invention of television, radio, or the Internet, this meant the Stamp Act taxed nearly every form of communication among the people. Outraged by this taxation without representation, the colonists engaged in protests and riots up and down the east coast. As part of this resistance, shop owners, artisans, farmers, and other colonists created clandestine groups that would become known as the Sons of Liberty, and in the late summer of 1765 they gathered at a large century old elm tree in front of Deacon Elliott's house in Boston and hung in effigy Andrew Oliver, the man appointed by Parliament to enact the Stamp Act tax on the colonists. Because of the colonists' defiance, the Stamp Act was repealed by Parliament in 1776, thus leading to celebrations at what was now called the Liberty Tree, where colonists filled it with streamers, flags, and lanterns. However, nine years later, in the summer of 1775, the American Revolutionary War had begun, and British soldiers and Loyalists under siege in Boston took their axes to the mighty Liberty Tree and felled it. Though now only a stump, the colonists would still gather around it to commemorate their victory against the Stamp Act and their role in fighting for America's freedom.

You'll find a nod to the original Liberty Tree on the walkway just behind the Ye Olde Christmas Shoppe, where the tree's stump sits just on the other side of a short railing.

www.Disney-Secrets.com

THE LIBERTY BELL

Found near the Liberty Tree is a life-sized replica of the historic Liberty Bell, the original of which hangs today in the Liberty Bell Center in Independence National Historical Park in Philadelphia, Pennsylvania. Around the top of the bell are the words...

PROCLAIM LIBERTY THROUGHOUT ALL THE LAND UNTO ALL THE INHABITANTS THEREOF LEV. XXV. V X – BY ORDER OF THE ASSEMBLY OF THE PROVINCE OF PENSYLVANIA FOR THE STATE HOUSE IN PHILAD.A

Astute guests will notice that the word "Pensylvania" appears to be misspelled on the bell. However, this isn't a mistake, but instead it's another example of Disney's level of attention to historical detail found throughout Liberty Square.

So how did this spelling come about originally?

In 1751, the Pennsylvania Assembly sought to obtain a large bell that could be heard all throughout the small but growing town of Philadelphia, as the current bell, purportedly brought to America by William Penn and hung in a tree outside the meeting place of the Pennsylvania colonial assembly, was proving to be too small to be heard to the town's limits when rung. In turn, the Assembly commissioned London's Whitechapel Bell Foundry to cast the new bell, which was to be known as the Pennsylvania State House Bell. Messrs. Isaac Norris, Thomas Leech and Edward Warner all signed the commission for the bell and directed that it should be "...shipped with the following words well shaped in large letters round it viz"...

BY order of the Assembly of the Province of Pensylvania for the State house in the City of Philad.a 1752 - Proclaim Liberty thro' all the Land to all the inhabitants thereof Levit. XXV. 10.

So at the hand of Messers. Norris, Leech and Warner the spelling of Pensylvania with only two "n"s originated, as this was considered to be an acceptable spelling of the word at that time.

Shortly after the bell's arrival in Philadelphia, it was discovered that the bell had suffered a crack, either in transit to America or upon its first ringing. Instead of having the bell shipped back to the Whitechapel Foundry, the Pennsylvania Assembly commissioned two Philadelphia men, John Pass and John Stow, to create an entirely new bell using the metal of the original one. Lacking the proper facilities of the Whitechapel Foundry, the two men broke the original bell into smaller pieces, melted them down and then recast the new bell with a similar design, though with a slightly different inscription, which read:

PROCLAIM LIBERTY THROUGHOUT ALL THE LAND UNTO ALL THE

INHABITANTS THEREOF LEV. XXV. V X – BY ORDER OF THE

ASSEMBLY OF THE PROVINCE OF PENSYLVANIA FOR THE STATE

HOUSE IN PHILAD.A

PASS AND STOW
PHILAD.A
MDCCLIII

Upon the new bell's completion, it was hung in the tower of the State House, later known as Independence Hall. However, the citizens did not like the tone of the new bell at all, so they requested Pass and Stow recast the bell once again. The second casting was a success, and it was this second bell that would go on to become known worldwide as the Liberty Bell.

It is interesting to note that many Liberty Bell replicas make the claim that they were cast from the same mold as the original Liberty Bell of either 1751 or 1752. However, this is highly unlikely, as bells manufactured in the mid-1700s were cast using fragile molds made of clay, horse hair, loam and horse manure, and in the case of the Pass and Stow bell, the mold using these elements was formed within a hole dug into the ground. Because the original 1751 bell and the ensuing Pass and Stow bell of 1752 had not achieved historical significance at the time of their casting, it is highly unlikely that much thought would have been given at the time to keeping either of these original fragile molds, let alone arranging to have them preserved for well over 200 years so they may be used in the 20th century. If this were to have occurred, then these same molds would still be preserved today, yet the molds, or even photos of them, do not exist.

Part of the confusion arises from a number of replicas made of the 1752 Pass and Stow bell. In 1950, President Harry Truman created a savings bond campaign to pay for the casting of approximately 56 Liberty Bell replicas by the Paccard Fonderie in Annecy Le Vieux, France. These replicas were from

22 New Liberty Bell Replicas – 1950 – Paccard Fonderie, France

all new molds, using the Pass and Stow Liberty Bell as a *guide*, and because they were created by the large and well-equipped Paccard Foundry in 1950 instead of two men in a small foundry in 1752, the bells exhibited a more polished and refined exterior, differing greatly from the somewhat crude and rough exterior of the original Pass and Stow Liberty Bell. Guests will notice that the Liberty Square Liberty Bell, which was cast in 1989, reflects the more refined exterior of its contemporary casting.

Source: Interview with Robert Giannini III – Museum Curator – Independence National Historical Park – Philadelphia, PA

"The Liberty Bell of Independence National Historical Park: A Special History Study – John C. Paige.

Liberty Bell photo courtesy of WDWGuidedTours.com

HISTORICAL FIRE PROTECTION

If you make your way down a short alleyway between the Columbia Harbour House and the Hall of Presidents, you'll find affixed above two large garage doors an interesting plaque consisting of four hands grasping wrists set on a wooden shield. More than just a piece of art, this is yet another reflection of the Imagineers' attention to historical detail.

During the mid-1700s, building owners in Philadelphia could purchase fire insurance and, in turn, receive a "fire mark" such as this, which they would then affix on the exterior of their building, between the first and second floor. Upon completing their fire fighting efforts, volunteer fire departments would then bill the insurance company depicted on the fire mark. Note: This fire mark belongs to Philadelphia's first fire insurance company, the Philadelphia Contributionship.

THEY'RE "DOVECOTES"

Above the fire mark, you'll notice four bird houses. Collectively, this is known as a "dovecote" or "pigeonaire". A tradition reaching back to medieval times throughout Europe, ancient Rome, and the Middle East, homeowners would build these into their homes or as elaborate freestanding structures so as to attract doves or pigeons, whose eggs were then used as an important food source.

CLEARLY MORE IMAGINEERING DETAIL

Now notice the number of small windows found throughout Liberty Square. As with Frontierland and Main Street, U.S.A., these windows reflect the Imagineers' commitment to the architecture and period-specific construction techniques available at the time these Lands represent. Contrary to the single larger panes of glass used throughout Tomorrowland, the windows here are small and numerous, as the ability to produce and transport large and expensive panes of glass wasn't available during the colonial period.

Now take a look at the construction technique used with each window. Notice how the Imagineers chose not to use modern window framing methods, but instead chose to use old-fashioned techniques by installing these windows using hand-applied window glazing, or putty. In nearby Frontierland, where supplies such as window glazing were difficult to come by in the old west, the windows are instead typically held in place with simple wood framing.

It's *clear* to see the Imagineers were dedicated to the period-specific details.

A Commitment to Detail

Now take a moment to notice the address numbers, hinges and other ornamentation on the buildings of Liberty Square for another subtle and often overlooked attention to detail. It would've been far easier for the Imagineers to simply install modern day address numbers, hinges and other ornamentation, but instead they chose to go the extra distance by installing items with the rough textured look of actual forged iron.  Did you also notice that instead of obtaining perhaps a dozen door knockers of the same design, the Imagineers outfitted each of the doors in Liberty Square with a different door knocker to reflect that the individual building owners each chose their own design?

Sit For a Spell

Want to sit for a spell and take a break during the Revolutionary War? Find the two large rocking chairs under the portico just to the right of the Hall of Presidents and enjoy a shady spot away from the noisy protests, rebellions, boycotts, and tea parties.

Debunking a Myth

 You'll often read that the Presidential Seal that greets guests inside the Hall of Presidents is one of only two official seals allowed for use outside of the White House. This is actually untrue. While the seal displayed here is *similar* to the official seal, it is substantially different in a number of ways.

Liberty Square Riverboat

Have you ever looked up at the Captain of the Liberty Square Riverboat in the wheelhouse and thought it would be such a magical experience to ride up there, as well? Here's how you can!

Be among the first to board the Liberty Square Riverboat and ask a Cast Member if you may join the Captain in the wheelhouse. There's a good chance you'll be granted permission to do so. You'll then make your way mid-deck and open the door that leads to the Captain's Quarters. Inside, you'll discover a fascinating, albeit small, area of the ship that is rarely seen by guests. Now climb the steep narrow stairs and join the Captain. Soon, the grand ship will cast its lines and you'll be underway on the Rivers of America. Be sure to

sound the Liberty Belle's iconic steam whistle if you see Tom and Huck fishing on the shore, and don't forget to ask about receiving an official Riverboat Co-Pilot's license that's given to guests who help pilot the magnificent vessel.

AN ALL NEW PERSPECTIVE

This next secret, while simple, is one that many guests miss because they think it's only a "boat ride", but it's far more than that.

Board the Liberty Square Riverboat and find a place on the front railing of the top deck. From here, you'll experience Frontierland, Big Thunder Mountain Railroad, Tom Sawyer Island and more, including a great view of the Haunted Mansion, from an entirely new and moving perspective.

You will also see story elements tucked along the shore that can be seen only from the Liberty Belle, something all the "landlubbers" will never experience!

THE HAUNTED MANSION

As you approach the Haunted Mansion, you'll notice a horseless funeral carriage out front. It's horseless in that the horse is there...but it isn't. Disney Imagineers continue the story of the Haunted Mansion well beyond the mansion itself with this creative story element mixed with the use of "themed paving". Look down and you will notice the horse's hoof prints are imprinted into the pavement and stretch from the carriage house out front to its final resting place beyond.

Beware of Bad Luck

Ninety-nine percent of guests miss this next secret, but you'll be lucky enough to see it...or will you?

Up near the rafters in the carriage house out front, you'll notice a number of horseshoes hanging from a set of metal hooks. Horseshoes are to be hung with the ends facing up, so as to catch and hold good luck. Unfortunately, all of these horseshoes are hung with the ends facing down, signifying that all of your good luck has run out...just as you are about to enter the Haunted Mansion.

Nightly Apparitions

From the horseless carriage to the pet cemetery, the Haunted Mansion experience begins well before guests enter the stretching room.

Those who visit the attraction at night will notice a story element that is missing during the day. Once it gets dark, stop in the queue line across from the front door of the mansion and watch the first and second story windows near the door. It may take a moment, but if you wait long enough, you'll see the shadow of a mysterious figure slowly passing behind one of the windows.

THEIR TIME IS NEAR

This next secret is a bit of a light-hearted one, but a key element in telling the story of the Haunted Mansion. Pause for a moment in the queue and look at the lawn, as well as the plants in the large planters near the mansion itself. Notice anything different here?

Disney horticulturists are some of the finest in the world, and they go to great lengths to ensure the landscaping all throughout Walt Disney World Resort is impeccable, be it at the Magic Kingdom or your hotel. Topiaries are shaped into whimsical Disney characters, flowers are blooming throughout the year, and every plant you see is green, lush and well-tended. However, here the horticulturists have purposely neglected the lawn and assorted plants of the Haunted Mansion so that they are brown, spindly...and barely clinging to life.

THEY'RE CHESS PIECES

Look at the roofline of the Haunted Mansion and you'll notice that it is adorned with oversized chess pieces. Here, you'll find the Queen, Rooks, Bishops, and Pawns ready for their match.

A Persistent Ring

Here's a Haunted Mansion secret that was buried...but wouldn't die.

Years ago, a turnstile at the exit of The Haunted Mansion was removed by Disney Imagineers. Part of this turnstile involved a support pipe about the diameter of a finger, and when this pipe was cut flush at its base, it left a "ring" in the pavement, a ring that soon took on a life of its own. Guests noticing the "ring" surmised that this was a wedding ring that belonged to the Bride. No doubt it was crushed here in a moment of rage, jealousy or perhaps even murder! Since this was not part of the official Haunted Mansion story, but instead only a tale that endured as legend and myth, Disney eventually paved over this piece of pipe when reimagining the queue line. However, with the disappearance of the Bride's ring, Disney guests became as enraged as Master Gracey, and a great howl was heard from Haunted Mansion fans across the globe. Disney, in a nod to this guest-inspired story and legend, created a more realistic ring and embedded it into the new interactive queue line. Can you find it? It's on the ground near the base of a short brick pillar on the other side of the brick wall behind the busts for The Twins, Wellington & Forsythia.

A Ghoulish Storm

As you journey through The Haunted Mansion, you'll notice its storyline takes place during a storm. Guests who visit the attraction at night will also notice that the same storm that thunders in scenes inside is carried outside as lightning periodically flashes and thunder rumbles across the mansion's facade.

MADAME LEOTA IS HAVING A BALL

The Imagineers are always innovating, and they've added a fun twist to a Magic Kingdom classic, the tombstones at the Haunted Mansion.

Step into the queue line and move to the front, just outside the main entrance doors. To your left, you'll spot a number of tombstones, each with a witty epitaph paying tribute to one of the designers, developers and artists who originally created the attraction. However, one tombstone, which honors the late Imagineer Leota Toombs Thomas, is unlike any other. Keep an eye on it and you'll soon notice the face will begin to "stretch" and move. Suddenly, the eyes open, look around and then close, often frightening those who are caught unaware!

Her epitaph reads:

> DEAR SWEET LEOTA
> BELOVED BY ALL
> IN REGIONS BEYOND NOW
> BUT HAVING A BALL

Leota Toombs Thomas was a Disney Imagineer who worked creating attraction figures, such as the animals for The Jungle Cruise, the birds of The Enchanted Tiki Room, and the ghosts of the Haunted Mansion. As an homage to Leota, the Imagineers chose to use her face as the image of the disembodied head within the crystal ball in the Haunted Mansion's seance scene, hence the reference on her tombstone to her "having a ball". *Photos courtesy of WDWGuidedTours.com*

"START TO
SHRIEK AND HARMONIZE"

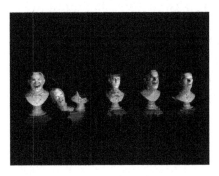

The quintet of singing busts in the lively graveyard scene, the ones singing "Grim Grinning Ghosts"? They all have names, and they are, from left to right, Rollo Rumkin, Uncle Theodore, Cousin Algernon, Ned Nub and Phineas P. Pock.

Note: Some guests incorrectly assume the "Uncle Theodore" bust is of Walt Disney, but it is actually of Thurl Ravenscroft, who had a bit of a resemblance to Walt. You can hear Mr. Ravenscroft's voice in many Disney productions and attractions, including Pirates of the Caribbean, The Enchanted Tiki Room and, of course, the Haunted Mansion. *Photo courtesy of WDWGuidedTours.com*

YOUR THREE
NEW GHOUL FRIENDS

The names of the three hitchhiking ghosts at the end of the attraction?. . . Phineas, Ezra and Gus.

HAUNTED MANSION PET CEMETERY

When exiting The Haunted Mansion, most guests make the mistake of passing too quickly by the wall at the mausoleum and the pet cemetery. Take a moment to stop and enjoy a ghoulish delight while others are rushing off to the next attraction.

In the early 1980s, Disney Imagineer Kim Irvine, daughter of Leota Toombs Thomas, had the idea of using the rarely-seen side lawn of Disneyland's Haunted Mansion as a pet cemetery. Using off-the-shelf statuary, she worked with fellow Imagineer Chris  Goosman to adorn each tombstone with witty epitaphs for such beloved pets as "Miss Kitty", "Bully" and "Big Jake". This new addition proved to be very popular with guests, so much so that Walt Disney Imagineering decided to add a larger pet cemetery in the front yard of the Haunted Mansion in 1993, where it has been light-heartedly haunting guests ever since. Realizing the 999 ghosts at Walt Disney World cared for their beloved pets, as well, the Imagineers brought this story element to the Magic Kingdom's Haunted Mansion where it resides on a hill behind a wrought iron fence.

I'd like to thank Disneyland Haunted Mansion historian Jeff Baham, author of *The Unauthorized Story of Walt Disney's Haunted Mansion,* for this story.

Big Jake and Rover

Within the pet cemetery guests will find a tombstone for Rover, a faithful dog who passed away in 1898, well over 120 years ago. His epitaph reads...

Every Dog Has His Day
Too Bad Today is Your Day

If you're thinking the tombstone for Rover looks familiar, you're right, as here the Imagineers have chosen to place a tombstone which is nearly identical, though not exactly, to the tombstone found for another dog, Big Jake, at Disneyland's Haunted Mansion. Though 3,000 miles apart, these two tombstones eerily bookend the Magic Kingdom and Disneyland pet cemeteries.

One Wild Ride Too Many?

Throughout the Magic Kingdom, guests will find the Disney Imagineers have hidden small tributes to former attractions. Stop and look carefully at the pet cemetery and notice the small statue of Mr. Toad. This was placed as a tribute to a Fantasyland attraction which is "no longer with us", Mr. Toad's Wild Ride.

LET THIS SECRET SINK IN

Those tombstones aren't leaning because of neglect on the Imagineers' part, they're leaning that way on purpose. As the story goes, each tombstone was standing straight on the day it was placed, but as the coffin below began to *deteriorate and decompose,* the ground began to give way, causing the tombstones to settle and lean.

MADAME LEOTA AND FRIENDS

After visiting the Haunted Mansion, make your way into the nearby Memento Mori shop and find an intricately carved oval framed mirror hanging on a wall. It may take a few moments, but if you're patient and deathly still, you'll soon be visited by an apparition of Madame Leota. She's not the only ghost in the shop, however. Tucked amongst a collection of old items up on some shelves are two large dusty jars. Watch them for a while and you'll see that they are actually home to a couple of spirits from regions beyond!

DON'T FORGET

By the way, "Memento Mori" is Latin for...

"Remember that you must die."

A GHOULISHLY GREAT VIEW

Getting a good view and a great picture of the Haunted Mansion can be difficult. Standing outside the queue in Liberty Square gives you only an oblique partial view of the place, while much of the mansion is obscured with the canopy while standing in the  queue itself. Here are two spots from which to get classic unobstructed photos...

1) Make your way to Aunt Polly's dock on Tom Sawyer Island. There, you'll find a perfect unobstructed view of the mansion, including its front door.

2) Board the Liberty Square Riverboat and make your way to the upper deck on its port (left) side. As the boat comes around and begins its approach to its mooring dock, another great view will begin to materialize, causing you to shriek and perhaps even harmonize with delight.

A WDW Guided Tours Tip:

Liberty Square features the best quick service spot for seating availability at Magic Kingdom. Head upstairs in the Columbia Harbour House restaurant to find an open table, even on the busiest of days!

Courtesy of WDWGuidedTours.com

www.Disney-Secrets.com

CHAPTER EIGHT

SECRETS OF FANTASYLAND

"Here is the world of imagination, hopes, and dreams. In this timeless land of enchantment, the age of chivalry, magic, and make-believe are reborn – and fairy tales come true. Fantasyland is dedicated to the young-in-heart, to those who believe that when you wish upon a star, your dreams come true."

- Walt Disney

WALT AND MICKEY

In a way, the "Partners" statue of Walt and Mickey in the hub in front of Cinderella Castle is the magical center of the park. Unknown to most guests, however, the statue you see here is not the original design. According to Disney, Blaine Gibson, who created the statue, initially sculpted it with Mickey holding a small ice cream cone. However, when they reviewed the statue, they felt it looked a little bit too much like Walt was taking his child out for a walk. To make Walt and Mickey look more like "Partners", Blaine took away the ice cream cone, and the end result is what you see in Disney parks across the world today.

TOWERING CINDERELLA CASTLE

Cinderella Castle is an excellent example of the concept of forced perspective, which the Imagineers use to make it appear much taller than its 189-foot height. If guests look closely, they'll notice the scale of the architectural elements and stonework get much smaller as the eye leads higher. For example, the dimensions of the stones at the base of the castle are larger than those up higher, and the railings used at the top of the spire are only two feet tall, a full one and a half feet shorter than other railings used at ground level throughout the parks.

AN AMAZING WORK OF ART

Just as with the windows on Main Street, U.S.A., the delicious Dole Whip, and Madame Leota's tombstone at the entrance to the Haunted Mansion, many guests rush right past magical Magic Kingdom story elements without ever realizing they exist.  This next secret is a classic that perhaps 99% of guests miss as they rush to and from the attractions of Fantasyland, but you'll want to make sure you're one of the 1% who stop and admire it.

Covering one side of the breezeway of Cinderella Castle is a stunning intricately hand-crafted work of art comprised of five large murals tucked amongst stately gothic arches. Here, over *one million* hand-cut glass, gold, silver, and jewel tiles come together in a radiant symphony of over 500 colors to tell the classic story of Cinderella. Disney Legend Dorthea Redmond and artists Hanns Scharff, along with his daughter-in-law Monika Scharf and six artisans, painstakingly assembled the murals over a period of two years to bring the story to life

with a vibrancy that can never be diminished.  Stop here to not only relive the story, but to study and appreciate the countless small details the artists have included within their work. While doing so, be sure to also see Cinderella's friends, who are carved into the gothic capitals lining the breezeway.

A Tribute to Two Imagineers

Here's another great hidden tribute to two notable Disney Imagineers.

While studying the impressive tile murals in the breezeway of Cinderella Castle, find the mural of Cinderella trying on the glass slipper. The two subjects at her feet are not fictional characters, but instead portray two actual Disney Imagineers; theme park and character designer John Hench (standing) and noted Disney artist and illustrator Herb Ryman.

Mad About the Details

Now find the images of Cinderella's two stepsisters in that scene, Anastasia and Drizella. Look closely and you'll notice the artists painstakingly portrayed their faces with green and red tiles to reflect them being green with envy and red with rage.

www.Disney-Secrets.com

CINDERELLA'S FRIENDS

Observant guests will notice the two mice watching from a ledge above in the receiving line area for Cinderella's Royal Table. They're friends of Cinderella, and their names are Jaq and Gus, from the 1950 animated Disney film, *Cinderella*.

THE ROYALTY OF CINDERELLA

Upon exiting Cinderella Castle and entering Fantasyland, look to the left to discover a small fountain and statue of Cinderella with a bird alight on her hand. A curtsey to the princess reveals a crown placed upon her head, depicted by the painted mural behind her. It is interesting to note, however, that Cinderella is never portrayed in Disney films or stories as wearing a crown. Perhaps this scene is to indicate her position as royalty?

SIGHT TINKER BELL IN KEEP

Happily Ever After is the spectacular fireworks performance that lights up the night sky in a dramatic pyrotechnic display high above Cinderella Castle, all scored to classic Disney songs, which play while scenes from your favorite Disney movies are projected on the castle's façade in an inspiring performance. Be sure not to leave before it's all over, however, as you'll want to see Tinker Bell take to the night sky in a daring flight as the spectacle begins to come to a close.

Prior to Tinker Bell's flight, and while all the other guests' eyes are attracted to the captivating fireworks, study the highest balcony atop the tallest keep (tower) of Cinderella Castle and you'll notice Tinker Bell standing in the dark while preparing for her entrance. Soon, she begins to brilliantly glow before taking flight to the amazement of everyone below!

THE DISNEY COAT OF ARMS

Before journeying through Cinderella Castle, take a moment to find the Coat of Arms posted over the front and rear entrances, as well as elsewhere nearby. With three lions arranged vertically and with their right forepaws raised, these are the Coat of Arms for the Disney family.

A GOODNIGHT
WISH FROM CINDERELLA

This next secret is one the vast majority of guests miss, yet it unveils for you a special magical moment in the Magic Kingdom.

Every night, guests hurry out of the park so as to be gone by the published park closing time. It can be a bit of a hurried experience as they rush to catch their transportation back to their resort. However, unknown to many, guests actually have one hour after the published closing time in which to make their way toward Main Street, U.S.A. and the exits. During this "twilight hour," make your way toward Cinderella Castle, find a bench, and take a moment to watch as it slowly adorns itself in a variety of constantly changing colors while saying goodnight to another enchanting day in the Magic Kingdom. This is also one of the best times of the day in which to capture photos of Cinderella Castle, Tomorrowland and Main Street, U.S.A., as each is lit in a variety of colors and very few guests are in the foreground.

Tip: Think you'll somehow miss your bus and have to walk back to your hotel if you stay too long at the Magic Kingdom? Rest assured...Disney buses run up to two hours after the park closes, and the final bus is not allowed to leave until the park is cleared of all guests and the final OK is given by Security.

PRINCE CHARMING REGAL CARROUSEL

Now make your way toward the Prince Charming Regal Carrousel to find Cinderella's favorite carrousel horse.

Originally built in 1917, the Prince Charming Regal Carrousel (formerly Cinderella's Golden Carrousel)  started its life as "Liberty" at Detroit Place Garden Park. In time, it was refurbished and moved to Olympic Park in Maplewood, New Jersey, before it was purchased by Disney in 1967 in anticipation of the opening of Walt Disney World Resort. It was then restored by the Disney Imagineers and has been enjoyed by park guests since opening day on October 1, 1971.

There are 86 horses on the Prince Charming Regal Carrousel, but only one has a gold ribbon on its tail. Park legend has it that this horse is Cinderella's favorite.

Tip: Guests have only a short time to pick and mount a horse once they are allowed onto the carrousel, so knowing what Cinderella's favorite horse looks like *before* you get on the carrousel will help you find it quickly once your turn to ride comes, as well as help prevent any possible meltdowns involving young guests. The way to do so is to watch the carrousel horses before you get in line so as to learn how to spot Cinderella's favorite horse when you board the attraction.

A HIDDEN TRIBUTE

Stand outside the exit for Peter Pan's Flight, and you'll notice a large wooden barrel off to one side labeled "Lost Boys Fire Brigade", along with the name of the Fire Chief. As with the windows that line Main Street, U.S.A., this barrel pays tribute to someone who plays an important role at Walt Disney World, the Fire Chief of the Reedy Creek Fire Department, the fire department charged with keeping all of Walt Disney World safe. However, unlike the windows of Main Street, U.S.A., the name painted on this barrel pays tribute to the *current* Fire Chief, and when this position changes hands, so does the name that appears on the barrel!

Note: The reason this barrel references the Lost Boys Fire Brigade is because it hides a fire hydrant.

ALL SIGNS POINT TO FUN

It's time for both lunch and an interactive secret! After ordering your meal at the Pinocchio Village Haus, find yourself a table at the windows on the west side of the restaurant that overlook the boarding area for the "it's a small world" attraction. It's fun to watch guests as they disappear nto a tunnel while anticipating the colorful and melodious world they're about to enter, but it is even more fun to interact with them from your seat. Find the set of oval cards that should be on one of the tables in the area, choose one with a "command" that you like, and then hold it up to the guests as they float by below and see how well they respond. Commands include *Clap Your Hands!*, *Touch Your Nose!*, *Say M-I-C-K-E-Y M-O-U-S-E!*, and more.

A HIDDEN NAUTILUS

As you make your way through the standby queue for Under the Sea – Journey of The Little Mermaid, you'll find a tribute to the attraction that used to occupy this space in the form of a Hidden Mickey, or in this case, a Hidden Nautilus. Cleverly carved into  the stonework on the other side of a small pool to the left, just before the drinking fountains, is an image of the Nautilus, Jules Verne's futuristic submarine featured in both the 1954 Disney classic, *20,000 Leagues Under the Sea*, as well as the former Fantasyland attraction.

REMEMBER NOVEMBER 18TH

This next secret reveals a rare Hidden Mickey that appears very briefly only once a year. As a result, very few guests ever get to see it. On the Under the Sea - Journey of The Little Mermaid attraction, the Imagineers have cleverly included a 3-circle notch in the rock formations of the queue that is aligned such that on November 18th...Mickey Mouse's birthday...the sun shines through the notch to form a three-circle Hidden Mickey for only a few minutes right at noon. That's it above, shining at the base of the queue line wall. My thanks to Dave Drumheller, for providing the perfectly timed photo.

Note: According to the Disney Archives, Mickey Mouse's birthdate *"...has always been determined to be the date that Steamboat Willie opened at the Colony Theater."*, which was November 18, 1928.

A SECRET AMONGST THE WHOSITS & WHATSITS

A little further along in the queue for Under the Sea – Journey of The Little Mermaid, you'll find some small caverns, each holding a collection of whosits and whatsits, gadgets and gizmos, thingamabobs, and treasures untold. Don't pass by these too quickly. Stop and watch any of the large jars that are stored here, or perhaps peer into a small window for a spell, and you'll soon be visited by someone who wants to be part of your world!

THE MANY ADVENTURES OF WINNIE THE POOH

Prior to the opening of The Many Adventures of Winnie the Pooh, the space was home to Mr. Toad's Wild Ride, a rollicking automobile adventure through the streets of London. As a tribute to this popular attraction, Disney Imagineers hung a picture in  The Many Adventures of Winnie the Pooh of Mr. Toad handing the deed of this attraction to Owl. In addition, as if to recognize his "demise", they placed a statue of Mr. Toad in the pet cemetery of the Haunted Mansion.

SEVEN DWARFS MINE TRAIN

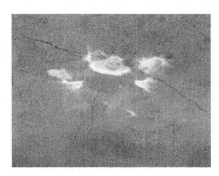 This next secret is kind of tricky to execute, as it relies upon a number of guests all cooperating at once. As you make your way through the queue of the Seven Dwarfs Mine Train, you'll come across a number of fun interactive queue activities. One of these consists of a collection of seven barrels filled with colorful gleaming diamonds. When you spin a barrel, one of the Seven Dwarfs appears as a projection on the ceiling above, but if you spin all seven barrels at once, thus projecting all seven of the

dwarfs on the ceiling at the same time, Snow White will then appear in the center of the projections, where she twirls briefly before disappearing.

A NOD TO A SCARY ADVENTURE

Disney Imagineers have carried on the tradition of honoring former attractions in another of the Magic Kingdom's attractions, the Seven Dwarfs Mine Train.

Along the train's course you'll spot a tall crane. Recognize the two vultures perched menacingly atop it? They are from the classic "dark ride" and guest favorite, Snow White's Scary Adventures, which existed from the park's opening day on October 1, 1971 until May 31, 2012. It was closed as part of the extensive Fantasyland expansion, and the Snow White story is now portrayed in the exciting Seven Dwarfs Mine Train. In addition to these two characters, five of the Seven Dwarfs used in Snow White's Scary Adventures appear in the attraction, and these are Bashful, Doc, Grumpy, Happy and Sleepy. Look for them inside the cottage at the end of the ride, just before disembarking.

A TRIBUTE TO WALT

In 1950, Walt Disney built in the backyard of his Holmby Hills, CA home a 1/8 scale railroad featuring a live-steam replica of the Central Pacific #173 locomotive, which he named the *Lilly Belle*, after his wife, Lillian. Winding its way along 2,600 feet of track, the locomotive and rolling stock passed over trestles, through a canyon, chugged past Walt's barn, and even disappeared into a tunnel that Walt had constructed under Lillian's prized roses. This was Walt's *Carolwood Pacific Railroad*, and the line was called *The Fairweather Route*.

While at the Fantasyland Railroad Station, look up above to see tributes to Walt, his Carolwood Pacific Railroad, and The

Fairweather Route. Here, you'll see Walt's initials placed at the peak of a gable, and behind it you'll find a large clock touting Carolwood Park and a Fairweather Place. Of course, it's all topped with a whimsical locomotive weathervane, all nod's to Walt and his love of trains.

To learn more about The Carolwood Pacific, I recommend you visit www.Carolwood.org. *Photo of Walt Disney used with permission from The Broggie Family Trust.*

LET THIS SECRET SOAK IN

Take a look at the four colorful and elaborate train cars of the Casey Jr. Splash 'N' Soak Station and you'll see that they each display a number. If you look at all of the numbers collectively, it'll slowly begin to soak in that these numbers weren't just chosen at random, but instead they represent the years in which the four parks of Walt Disney World opened, with the Magic Kingdom in 1971, Epcot in 1982, Disney's Hollywood Studios in 1989, and Disney's Animal Kingdom in 1998.

SIR MICKEY'S GIANT SECRET

He may be huge, but he's not easily seen. Stop in at Sir Mickey's Shop in Fantasyland and look up. There you'll find Willie the Giant from Mickey and the Beanstalk peeking in from under the roof.

"IT'S A SMALL WORLD"

Be sure to stop and enjoy the classic animated clock of "it's a small world" opposite the queue line as it puts on a show every quarter hour.

MAXIMUS
MAKES AN IMPRESSION

Themed paving used throughout the Magic Kingdom can get pretty creative, and just in front of Rapunzel's tower in Fantasyland you'll find that her horse, Maximus, has gotten in on the fun, as well. Look for his horseshoe prints in the concrete along the walkway. You'll know they're his, because his name is imprinted with every step.

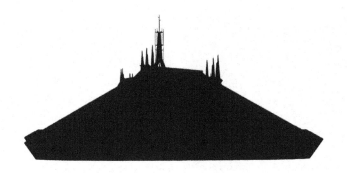

CHAPTER NINE

SECRETS OF TOMORROWLAND

"Tomorrow offers new frontiers in science, adventure, and ideals: the atomic age...the challenge of outer space...and the hope for a peaceful and unified world."

- Walt Disney

BUZZ LIGHTYEAR'S
SPACE RANGER SPIN

The next stop on your "Secrets Tour" brings you to the Winner's circle.

In Buzz Lightyear's Space Ranger Spin, guests compete against each other for the high score. It's fairly easy to rack up a *good* score, but if you want the big points and a chance to get to the coveted 999,999, then you have to know what to hit, as a handful of targets are worth 50,000 or 100,000 points each. Typically, the harder it is to hit the target, the more it's worth. Here are a few key targets...

- As you enter the room with the large orange robot, watch his right eye. (To your left) Once it begins blinking with an "X", it's worth 100,000 points.

- The menacing Zurg can be intimidating, but fire at a target at his base and you'll be rewarded with 100,000 points.

- Spot the volcano and fire on the target at the top. It is worth 50,000 points.

You have your mission, so blast away and help Buzz save the Galactic Empire from Evil Emperor Zurg! *Photo courtesy of WDWGuidedTours.com*

SPACE MOUNTAIN

Here's a tip that may give you a rare inside look at Space Mountain with the lights on.

If you're in Tomorrowland and Space Mountain is closed, chances are the lights are on inside as the Imagineers are performing some maintenance on the tracks. Walk over to the nearby Tomorrowland Transit Authority, which usually has a very short wait time of five minutes or less, and climb aboard a transport vehicle. The vehicle traverses *through* Space Mountain, so you'll get an inside look at the attraction with the lights on as you travel along.

Note: Does Space Mountain in the Magic Kingdom look larger than its counterpart in Disneyland? That's because it is. Disneyland's Space Mountain is 200' in diameter, while the Magic Kingdom's comes in at 300'.

MONSTERS, INC. LAUGH FLOOR

This next secret has to do with being in the right place at the right time to be the right choice. During each performance of the Monsters, Inc. Laugh Floor, one person is selected from an audience of 400 guests to be "That Guy", someone the show highlights and teases repeatedly throughout the show, but all in a good-natured manner. For being a good sport, this one person is given a unique souvenir very few guests ever receive, their very own "*I was that guy at Monsters, Inc. Laugh Floor*" sticker! Photo courtesy of WDWGuidedTours.com

Only One Letter...
But 3,000 Miles...Apart

This next secret may not be out of this world, but it is kind of fun to know.

Pay attention and you'll notice the Magic Kingdom's "Astro Orbiter" attraction is known by a slightly different name at Disneyland. The difference is one single letter, with Disneyland's attraction known as the "Astro Orbitor".

The Magic Kingdom's Astro Orbiter initially opened as the Star Jets attraction in 1974, and it ran for twenty years before closing as part of Tomorrowland's extensive renovation in 1994. Reopening in 1995, the new attraction was renamed the "Astro Orbiter."

Disneyland's version of this attraction opened in July, 1967 as the Rocket Jets. Closing in 1997, it underwent a major renovation patterned after Disneyland Paris' Orbitron attraction, and as such, reopened in 1998 as the new Astro Orbitor.

Robo-Newz

After you exit the Tomorrowland Transit Authority, wander over to the entrance for the Astro Orbiter and look for the "Robo-Newz" robot featuring "up-to-the-minute" news. While only a prop, this high-tech robot "offers" newspapers printed while you wait. The latest edition of the Galaxy Gazette sports a headline which reads, *Stitch Escapes!*, a tie-in to the nearby Stitch's Great Escape!

METROPHONE

Now make your way to the nearby Metrophone. Brought to you by the Galactic Communications Network, this is a galactic phone booth offering toll free calls to anywhere in the galaxy. Make your selection on the dial and listen in on one of a few different interstellar calls!

A STYLING HIDDEN MICKEY

Hidden Mickeys are fun to spot anywhere, even in the future!

While you ride the Tomorrowland Transit Authority attraction, take note of the futuristic scene in which a woman is having her hair done while sitting with a large "styling device" over her entire head. Though somewhat difficult to see, if you study her belt, you'll see a 3-Circle Hidden Mickey.

A CAROUSEL OF HIDDEN MICKEYS

The classic Carousel of Progress holds a number of Hidden Mickeys, many of which can be found in the holiday scene. Look for Mickey in the small salt and pepper shakers on the kitchen counter over by dad, the large Mickey Mouse plush toy tucked amongst the presents under the Christmas tree, and, all the way to the left of the scene, a Hidden Mickey nutcracker set on the fireplace mantle.

SECRETS OF EPCOT'S FUTURE WORLD

But the most exciting and, by far, the most important part of our Florida project, in fact, the heart of everything we'll be doing in Disney World, will be our experimental prototype city of tomorrow. We call it EPCOT, spelled E-P-C-O-T: Experimental Prototype Community of Tomorrow. Here it is in larger scale. EPCOT will take its cue from the new ideas and new technologies that are now emerging from the creative centers of American industry. It will be a community of tomorrow that will never be completed, but will always be introducing testing and demonstrating new materials and new systems. And EPCOT will always be a showcase to the world of the ingenuity and imagination of American free enterprise.

- Walt Disney

SPACESHIP EARTH

Epcot's Spaceship Earth attraction takes guests on a journey through time as they marvel at scenes depicting the fascinating advancement of communication technology through the ages, from the invention of papyrus for written messages between men to today's digital signals transmitted between distant planets.

In 2008, Spaceship Earth underwent a significant reimagineering, and as part of that Disney Imagineers wanted to represent the era of telegraphy, captured in a scene in which a telegraph operator transmits the historical news of the ceremonial driving of the Golden Spike near Promontory Summit, Utah on May 10, 1869, thus completing the Transcontinental Railroad. To "plus" the scene, the Imagineers decided to have the sound of the Morse Code being tapped out by the telegraph operator be audible to guests as they traveled by in their vehicles, and to ensure its accuracy, it was further decided that this Morse Code would be in "American Morse", or "Railroad Morse", as it was also known, as this was the type of Morse Code used in that part of the country at that point in time. However, this presented a problem when it came to finding someone today who could tap out that message, as American Morse largely became extinct in the early 1900s after being replaced by International Morse Code.

In considering their options, one of the Imagineers, Glenn Barker, recalled a guest, Mr. George Eldridge, who had brought to his attention years before an error Mr. Eldridge had noticed in the Morse Code being tapped out for Walt Disney's Opening Day speech at the Disneyland Railroad New Orleans Square Station. Using his skillful ear and modern day technology, Mr. Eldridge worked with Mr. Barker to correct the error.

Realizing Mr. Eldridge could probably help the Imagineers solve this current problem, Mr. Barker contacted him and asked for his assistance. After getting up to speed on American Morse Code, Mr. Eldridge tapped out the message you hear today in the Spaceship Earth attraction, thus making him perhaps the only guest to have his work featured in an attraction in both Disneyland and Walt Disney World!

The message you hear being tapped out in the Spaceship Earth telegraphy scene...

PROMONTORY UTAH
GOLDEN SPIKE
RR CPT
USA CONNECTED

Where "RR CPT" is the Railway Telegraph abbreviation for "Railroad Complete.

Source: My interview with Mr. George Eldridge

Note: If the scene in the Spaceship Earth attraction is depicting the actual telegrapher at the scene of the Golden Spike ceremony, then the name of the telegrapher is Watson Shilling.

EAST MEETS WEST MEETS WALT

It's interesting to note that of the countless locomotive designs in use throughout history, the two steam locomotives used for the ceremonial driving of the Golden Spike at Promontory Summit, Utah were both similar in design to the Central Pacific #173, the steam locomotive that Walt Disney used as the inspiration for his miniature "Lilly Belle" steam engine, which he built and ran on his "Carolwood Pacific" railroad in the backyard of his Holmby Hills home. This miniature locomotive played an important role in Disney history and became the inspiration for all the train engines you see at Disney theme parks around the world today.

Above is a photo of Central Pacific #173, and to the right is a photo of a replica of one of the locomotives from the Golden Spike ceremony, the Jupiter, which is officially known as Central Pacific #60.

FUTURE WORLD EAST
& FUTURE WORLD WEST

Here's a secret most guests walk through, around and over without ever noticing. As you make your way into Future World, stop and notice the subtle difference in the architectural and landscaped features between Future World

East and Future World West. Future World East is a world of science and technology, and as such, the Imagineers conveyed this using construction with hard angles, straight pathways and geometrical features, whereas Future World West reflects more of the natural wonders of our planet, and this is represented in more free-flowing designs with softer edges, curved walkways, an abundance of plants and flowers, and, of course, plenty of water.

IT'S UPSIDE DOWN!

The center piece of the Imagination pavilion is all about imagination! Take a look at the large fountain in front of the glass pyramids and watch it for a while to see something truly creative. Here, water flows up instead of down, as if the entire fountain is an upside down waterfall!

JAMMIN' AT EPCOT

Walk right past that cleaning crew without stopping, and you may be making a big mistake.

When visiting Epcot, keep an eye out for a rather boisterous trio of janitors. At first glance, it may appear they're simply on their way to

do some cleaning, but stop and watch, because you're about to witness JAMMitors, a percussion group that mixes fast-paced percussion on trash cans with an interactive comedy filled performance. During Epcot's International Food & Wine Festival, you'll find this same group performing as the Jammin' Chefs on pots and pans over stoves.

TEST TRACK

Motor over to Test Track Presented by Chevrolet and climb into your own custom test vehicle to experience a nearly mile-long attraction at close to 65 m.p.h.. . . making it the longest and fastest attraction in all of Walt Disney World Resort.

YOU CAN KEEP RACING!

Tucked into the large exit area for Test Track are not only the newest cars on the market from Chevrolet, but also a collection of high-tech racing games where you take the wheel and compete against other drivers. There's no need to wait in the Test Track line

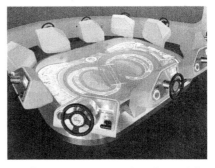

to play, either. Simply walk into the exit area via the wide walkway to the right of the Test Track entrance to test your high speed skills.

29 LANDING SPOTS

If you just head to the queue for Mission: SPACE without pausing outside first, then you'll miss out on all of the stellar achievements the Imagineers have paid tribute to in the forecourt of the attraction. Before you enter

Mission: SPACE, find the large model of the moon outside. There, on its surface, you'll find 29 indicators which represent the different landing sites used by astronauts and unmanned spacecraft between the years of 1959 and 1976.

IT'S ACTUALLY BEEN IN SPACE

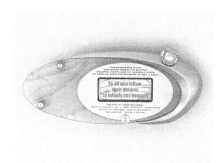

Also located in the forecourt of Mission: SPACE is a collection of plaques that pay tribute to the brave astronauts and notable achievements of the space program. One of these also pays tribute to Walt, those who dream, and even Buzz Lightyear!

Find the plaque that holds another plaque that flew into space aboard the Atlantis space shuttle during April 24, 2000 to May 4, 2000, and you'll find it reads...

To all who follow their dreams "to infinity and beyond!"

INSPIRATIONAL SECRETS

As you further explore the outer reaches of the entrance area to *Mission: SPACE*, take note of some of the special moments immortalized here. See the imprints of the tracks belonging to the two Mars rovers; Spirit and Opportunity, read inspirational quotes by

Stephen Hawking, U.S. Astronaut Barbara Morgan, and others, and admire again the words of Neil Armstrong spoken on July 20, 1969 when he stepped on the moon... *"That's one small step for man, one giant leap for mankind."*

THE LAND

In designing the entrance to The Land, the Imagineers wanted to convey to guests a sense of the bountiful, dynamic and powerful elements that make up our planet. Rows and rows of green plants of all kinds were planted to represent earth's natural riches and bounty, while trees flowering with white blossoms convey the essence of life-giving weather in the sky, and the layers of earth that have folded and heaved under tremendous forces beneath us are captured in the impressive tile mosaic at the entrance to the attraction.

CREATED BY
FRIENDS OF CINDERELLA

Speaking of the tile mosaic at the entrance to The Land, it's interesting to note that this mosaic was created by Hanns Scharff and his daughter-in-law, Monika, the same artists who created the five colorful mosaics that tell the story of Cinderella in the breezeway of the Magic Kingdom's Cinderella Castle.

DEBUNKING A COMMON MYTH

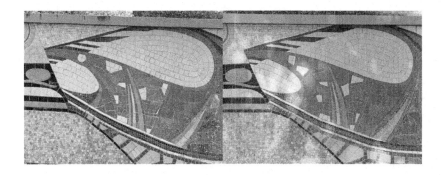

One of the common myths you read about the mosaic tile work at the entrance of The Land pavilion is that both sides leading to the entrance doors are *exactly* the same, tile for tile, except for one small tile on the sign for the pavilion. If you sit for a spell here and compare both sides, you'll see that, while both sides are of the *same design*, they are not exactly the same. In fact, they differ in a number of areas. Take a look at the two sections above, which appear on opposite sides of the entrance. Can you spot the many differences?

IT'S A VOLCANO

Here's a secret about The Land that most guests walk over and through without ever noticing. While standing at the sign for the pavilion, near the beginning of the two long tile mosaics, take note of how you're actually standing at the base of a slope that leads up to the entrance doors, a feature no other pavilion in Epcot has. This slope, combined with the story of the layers of the earth told through the mosaic, as well as the shape of the building itself reveals The Land pavilion to actually be a volcano!

GO BEHIND THE SEEDS

Guests can actually "dig deeper" into The Land.

Don't miss the opportunity to go beyond the exhibits and take a close look at the four greenhouses, fish farm, high-tech horticulture and more going on behind the scenes. The "Behind the Seeds" greenhouse tour is an intriguing 1 hour journey behind closed doors in which you will take an herb and spice challenge, feed fish at the fish farm, release some ladybugs, see record setting plants and more. Same day reservations can be made at the Tour Desk on the lower level of The Land or by calling 407-WDW-TOUR (407-939-8687) in advance.

A RECORD TOMATO TREE

An official Guinness World Record holding secret is up next at The Land pavilion.

A voyage on the Living with the Land boat ride reveals a record setting tomato tree that weighs over 1,100 pounds and produces more than 32,000 tomatoes in one year! In addition to the world record tomato tree, guests will also find a cucumber tree, nine-pound lemons, and Mickey Mouse shaped cucumbers, pumpkins, and watermelons.

www.Disney-Secrets.com

None of Their Beeswax

As you make your journey through Living with the Land, study the myriad plants, flowers, fruits and vegetables. Do you notice anything missing? It's an absolutely critical component required for plants to live, grow and thrive...yet you won't find it here. Give up? It's bees! Disney Imagineers knew that having guests floating through the attraction amidst thousands of busy bees could potentially be a problem, so they created the attraction without them. As a result, scientists spend about 15 hours every week hand pollinating the plants.

A Soarin' Hidden Mickey

While enjoying Soarin' Around the World, guests will discover two Hidden Mickeys. The first appears briefly when three colorful hot air balloons align for only a moment over the United State's desert southwest, while the second appears when fireworks burst high above Spaceship Earth.

The World's Largest Flower Bed

The immense flower bed you're walking past in Future World West? It happens to be the largest flower bed found in all of Walt Disney World Resort, and it holds over 20,000 plants.

THE SEAS WITH NEMO & FRIENDS

Did you know you can snorkel with the fish, rays, sea turtles and even sharks of The Seas with Nemo & Friends? Disney offers the 2.5 hour "Epcot Seas Aqua Tour" for those guests who don't have open water SCUBA certification.

Want to take it to the next level? If you have open water SCUBA certification, you can also scuba dive at The Seas with Nemo & Friends by taking part in the 3-hour "DiveQuest" tour.

Would you believe you can also swim with dolphins at Walt Disney World?! You can with Disney's "Dolphins in Depth." This 3-hour tour allows guests to get up close and interact with dolphins in knee-deep water.

Learn more about these tours and make reservations by calling 407-939-8687.

SECRETS OF EPCOT'S
WORLD SHOWCASE

"To all who come to this Place of Joy, Hope and Friendship, Welcome. EPCOT is inspired by Walt Disney's creative vision. Here, human achievements are celebrated through imagination, wonders of enterprise and concepts of a future that promises new and exciting benefits for all. May EPCOT Center entertain, inform and inspire, and, above all, may it instill a new sense of belief and pride in man's ability to shape a world that offers hope to people everywhere."

- Card Walker – Epcot Dedication

SHOWCASE PLAZA

Tucked to the right hand side of Showcase Plaza is a telescope right at the water's edge, just waiting to show you the world from an all new perspective.

While most guests enter World Showcase and rush off in the direction of either Mexico or Canada, those who break from the pack and proceed straight ahead will find an expansive view of World Showcase along with the telescope, which allows a unique close up view of each pavilion from a single location.

ELEVEN AND THEN SOME

In addition to the eleven pavilions you see today, there were an additional eight pavilions considered before the park opened. These were the African Nations pavilion, Costa Rica, Denmark, Iran, Israel, Spain, Switzerland and Venezuela.

DINE WITH THE FIREWORKS

The La Hacienda de San Angel restaurant at Epcot's Mexico pavilion is an excellent place from which to enjoy the fireworks over World Showcase Lagoon, as the restaurant was designed specifically to give guests an outstanding view of the fireworks during their dining. Reservations are encouraged.

On With The Show

Many guests incorrectly assume that the evening's fireworks over World Showcase Lagoon will be cancelled if it's raining, or it looks like it's going to rain, but this is incorrect. Fireworks performances are never cancelled due to rain, so if it  looks like there is going to be some precipitation during the show, then stick around, as all kinds of excellent viewing spots will begin to open up as other guests leave.

Tip: Fireworks performances will be cancelled due to high winds or if there is any lightning in the area, and the decision to cancel the performance is typically made shortly before its scheduled beginning. This is an important point to keep in mind if you are planning on leaving another park to head over to Epcot to see the show. If it is very windy or the possibility of lightning exists, then don't bother to make the trip.

Kidcot Fun Stops

When Epcot opened in 1982, the Imagineers soon realized its focus on science, technology and world attractions failed to generate the same kind of interest young children had in the Magic Kingdom, its characters and story elements. As a result, they began to develop new programs which would allow kids to interact with the park, and one of these was Kidcot Fun Stops, a journey filled with enchanting stops at each pavilion where children could decorate their own personal souvenir with the colors, trinkets and stamps of each country. Stop by a pavilion as you enter World Showcase and ask a Cast Member for a Kidcot Fun Stops souvenir.

You Can Talk to the World

One of the most amazing secrets you can discover while touring World Showcase are the Cast Members themselves. While many are from the local area or perhaps another state, others are from the very country which you are visiting and are more than happy to share about their home country, its culture, history, attributes, and why you should visit someday. Feel free to engage them in conversation and ask questions to unlock even more fascinating secrets about World Showcase.

Mexico

As you arrive at the Mexico pavilion study its iconic pyramid for another example of the same forced perspective Disney Imagineers use with Cinderella Castle, Expedition Everest and Main Street, U.S.A. While it appears much higher, the pyramid's total height is actually less than 50 feet.

Norway

Before exploring the Norway pavilion, stop for a moment out on the esplanade and stand where you can see all of the pavilion at once. While it's designed to look like a single small village, it also showcases a number of different regions of Norway through its architecture, which also serves to show a progression of time through the country's history.

Beginning on the left, you'll see the Royal Sommerhus Meet and Greet with Anna and Elsa. Representing the Setesdal valley in southern Norway, this cabin reflects an earlier period in which structures were built of logs, before progressing to the use of sawn lumber, thus allowing for more architectural details and expressions like those found on the impressive Stave church and quaint Kringla Bakeri og Kafe.

Continuing beyond the church, you'll discover the buildings of The Fjording, which reflect the famous Bryggen Street, known for its colorful collection of historic structures in the harbour district of Bergen, Norway. Take note of the two buildings that are joined, yet share one doorway, a distinct architectural feature that is common in Bryggen.

Next, as you step by the entrance to the Frozen attraction, you'll begin to see architecture reflecting the medieval period, as noted with the introduction of gothic elements, including pointed arches and small "rose windows", as well as stonework reminiscent of that found on the 14th century Akershus Castle, which stands today in Oslo, Norway's capitol.

NORWAY'S STAVE CHURCH

The majestic building at the center of the Norway pavilion? It's a 4/5-scale reproduction of Norway's 12th century Gol Stave Church in Hallingdal, Norway. According to Disney...*Named for their wooden stave planks, Norway's iconic stave churches were constructed using many of the same techniques used to build Norwegian ships. To help protect the medieval structures against the harsh winters, master craftsmen designed the*

churches with steep rooflines and elevated them onto stone foundations, which prevented the staves from rotting in the wet ground.

Many guests admire the church from outside, unaware that they are more than welcome to step inside to discover a fascinating museum displaying Norway's rich Viking heritage.

THE PATRON SAINT OF NORWAY

Before you venture inside the church, however, take note of the wooden statue out front. That is of Olaf Haraldsson, or "Saint Olaf", the Patron Saint of Norway.

IT'LL GROW ON YOU

While at the small Kringla Bakeri Og Kafe, take note of the special roof the Imagineers were sure to include on a few of the "older" buildings in the pavilion as a nod to a rather interesting piece of Norway's ancient heritage. While other buildings in the pavilion are roofed with stone, wood and tile, this small roof grows grass.

Comprised of approximately three inches of sod and covering a thin layer of long-lasting birch bark, which makes the roof waterproof, this construction technique has been used since before the time of the Vikings, as ancient Norwegians realized that such a roof is not only inexpensive, but also an excellent insulator in both hot and cold weather.

Now take note of the little metal railing affixed to the gutter. In another attention to detail, this railing's purpose is to keep any snow and ice from sliding off the roof and onto guests below. It is Norway, after all!

THAT'S A LOT OF ROOSTING

Next to the Kringla Bakeri Og Kafe is the Puffin's Roost, offering a selection of quality Norwegian apparel, souvenirs, curios and collectibles. Take note of the small carved Puffin above the door, which is a nod to the fact that Norway is home to 30% of the world's Atlantic Puffin population, the majority of which flock to northern Norway by the hundreds of thousands beginning in March of every year.

BRICKED UP WINDOWS

Now visit the tall round tower found at the south end of the pavilion, on the way to China. Study carefully the stone facade. Do you see the bricked up windows that do not match the stone? Surely the Disney Imagineers didn't make a mistake, which they then had to cover up, did they? No, not at all. This is actually yet another example of the Imagineers' attention to both detail and history.

Originating out of England's Lights and Windows tax of 1696, residents of Norway were in time assessed a tax based upon the number of windows in their home. Given glass was expensive, the tax assessors reasoned that the more windows in a residence, the more wealth and income the homeowner must have, so a tax on windows would not only be easy to determine, as one could simply count the windows from outside, but it would also be fair for all. However, Norwegians cleverly worked to evade this "window tax" by boarding or bricking up the windows they felt they could live without. In this case, it was the higher windows in the tower. *Photo courtesy of WDWGuidedTours.com*

HAT'S OFF TO A
CLASSIC THAT IS NO MORE

At one time, the Norway pavilion was home to the Maelstrom boat ride, as well as a Hidden Mickey known both far and wide. As with the Disney Imagineers' practice of paying respects to former attractions, I've decided to keep a reference to it within this book, even though it has now set sail. As guests stood in the queue for Norway's Maelstrom boat ride, they would've noticed a Viking boat on the left side of a large mural which depicted the history and wonders of Norway. There, in the middle of a crowded boat, was a perfect example of Disney Imagineering whimsy, as amidst all the battle-ready warriors was one lone Viking, painted by Imagineer Terry Peterson, wearing Mickey Mouse ears! And to top it all off, the name stitched on the front was "Leif". Truly classic. You can read more about how Terry came to paint this Hidden Mickey in the book *Disneyland In-Depth*.

Source: My interview with Terry Peterson

www.Disney-Secrets.com

CHINA

Now journey next door and see another attention to detail that is subtle, yet very important as an accurate portrayal of the host country.

Notice the water in the landscaping at the China pavilion. Here, as in China itself, water used in a landscape is typically still, whereas the water found in other pavilions, such as Japan, France, or Canada involves movement or flow, sometimes even as a waterfall.

PRINCE MIN

This next secret reveals a prince at Walt Disney World whom very few have ever heard of, yet he's there to be seen by tens of thousands of guests every day.

Venture to the China pavilion and find a small sculpture of a man atop a hen on the roofline of the Nine Dragons Restaurant. This man is Prince Min, a cruel 3rd century ruler who was hanged for his actions. His presence on the roof is a warning to all other tyrants to keep away, and the other animals behind him, including a fierce dragon, are there to keep him from escaping.

An Indication of Importance

Now take notice of some of the other rooflines within the China pavilion. Do you notice how some have sculptures similar to those with Prince Min, while others have fewer or none at all? Chinese citizens could gauge the importance and luxuriousness of the buildings of the Ch'ing Dynasty by the architecture employed, the use of red colored columns, and the number of sculptures placed on the rooflines, with the more sculptures placed, the more important the building and the business conducted therein, which was usually government related.

A Familiar Voice

Standing prominently within the pavilion is a half sized re-creation of the Hall of Prayer for Good Harvests, the original of which stands today in the Temple of Heaven imperial complex in Beijing, China. Of note is guests can stand at the very center of the intricately painted circular hall just inside the entrance doors and, as a testament to the acoustics of the hall, hear an echo of their voice. Go ahead and give it a try.

www.Disney-Secrets.com

ARCHITECTURE THROUGH THE YEARS

While not in a chronological progression like the United Kingdom or Norway pavilions, the China pavilion displays numerous designs of Chinese architecture from a period of a couple hundred years before the Ch'ing Dynasty to more contemporary facades using modern materials.

"WATER SPOUTING BASIN"

Now make your way toward the back of the China pavilion and step into the Yong Feng Shangdian shop. There, on a pedestal, is a large bronze basin with two handles, one which most guests assume to be a simple wash basin filled with water. This basin,

however, is unlike any you've ever seen before, as it is the Fish Basin, or "water-spouting" basin. The small sign above it reads...

"The fish basin is dated back to the song Dynasty (960 to 1279 A.D.). The bronze basin has two prominent handles and four fish in relief on the bottom, as well as a line emanating from the mouths or tails of the fish. When the handles are rubbed briskly with the palms of the hands, a harmonious sound is heard and standing waves are excited in the four quadrants along the circumference. Meanwhile a water column comes alive, spouting into the air, as if squirting from the four fish."

Rubbing your palms lengthwise along the handles creates a resonation that causes the water to "dance" in the four quadrants of the bowl. Note that rubbing your hands on the handles in a lateral outward and back motion does not create the same effect. Go ahead and give it a try!

BIRDS OF A FEATHER ROOST TOGETHER

Immediately after leaving the China pavilion, you'll cross a small bridge over a waterway. If your schedule allows for it today, then be sure to head back here this evening, just after the sun sets, and take note of the hundreds of birds that flock to the trees lining the waterway as they begin to settle in for the night. Light, dark, big, and small, they all roost on the branches in a natural spectacle that is amazing to watch.

COOLPOST

Stop at the Coolpost and lift the lids on the old-fashioned Coca-Cola coolers for a fun secret most guests walk right past.

SHE'S WISHING TO MEET YOU

Just before reaching the Germany pavilion, keep an eye out for Snow White on your left, as she can often be found here greeting guests next to her wishing well.

GERMANY

As you enter the Germany pavilion, take notice of the façade of Das Kaufhaus to your right. Here the Disney Imagineers have paid tribute to the historical Merchants' Hall of Freiburg im Breisgau, found in southwest Germany. Hundreds of years old now  and dating back to the 14th century, this impressive structure served as an important financial institution to the region.

Due to the space limitations of the Germany pavilion, the Imagineers elected to build this architectural replica approximately three-quarters the size of the original structure. As such, it is adorned with three statues, instead of the four found on the façade in Freiburg im Breisgau. But just who do these statues represent? They are a family of Monarchs and Emperors dating back to 1459! From left to right, you'll find...

Philip I of Castile

Born in July of 1478, Philip I of Castile, also known as Philip the Handsome, was the son of Emperor Maximilian I. Because he died before his father, he never became an emperor, but instead was the first Habsburg Monarch of Spain. And the item hanging on the "necklace" around his neck? That's a ram, and it represents the Distinguished Order of the Golden Fleece, a Catholic order of chivalry founded in 1430.

Emperor Charles V

Born in 1500, Charles V was the eldest son of Philip I of Castile. Becoming the ruler of the Netherlands at age 6, he ruled over a domain comprised of nearly four million square kilometers, ultimately assuming the role of Emperor from his grandfather, Maximilian I.

Ferdinand I

The younger brother of Charles V, Ferdinand I was born in March of 1503. As a Royal, he became King of Bohemia, Hungary and Croatia before becoming Emperor upon the death of his brother, Charles V, in 1558.

Missing from this collection of statues is the father of all three, Emperor Maximilian I, whom is depicted on the original facade to the left those you see here.

Note: Just for the fun of it, the small ornate "roof" you see above each statue's head is called a baldachin.

A ROYAL HIDDEN MICKEY

In another example of Imagineering whimsy, study the three statues adorning Das Kaufhaus and find the one sporting a crown with a Hidden Mickey front and center. Tip: You may find it easier to zoom in with your camera, which will then allow you to study the detail of the crown up close.

ST. GEORGE

While in the Germany pavilion, it's impossible to miss the dramatic statue in the middle of the platz. Here the Imagineers have paid tribute to St. George, the patron saint of soldiers, who slayed a dragon that was about to take the life of a King's daughter. Statues and artwork conveying this same story can be found throughout much of Germany, and while they all vary in their appearance and interpretation, all are quite impressive.

A CHIME TO REMEMBER

If you pass through the Germany pavilion too quickly, you'll most likely miss this next secret. Each hour, on the hour, the large glockenspiel, located beneath the clock at the back of the platz, or plaza, performs a unique chime composed especially for the pavilion, complete with two charming Hummel figurines who emerge from under a large ornate baldachin and strike a bell.

EPCOT'S GARDEN RAILWAY

The Magic Kingdom has the Walt Disney World Railroad, Disney's Animal Kingdom has the Wildlife Express, and Disney's Hollywood Studios has Minnie & Mickey's Runaway Railway, so it's only fitting that Epcot has a railway, too, and you'll  find it at the Germany pavilion. Here, the small G-scale trains of the Garden Railway ply the tracks through quaint Bavarian villages scattered across a bucolic countryside. It's very easy to overlook, as it's often screened with strollers as guests focus on making their way over to Italy, but take a moment to stroll along The Romantic Road and study all of the small details the Imagineers have included. Street musicians are playing outside the small village church, workmen are taking a break for lunch, a young couple are getting married, and of course, people are waiting at the train depot for the next train to arrive and take them over to Füssen.

Something to consider with the Garden Railway is that the villagers are always busy, and as a result, the scenery is constantly changing. While they may be throwing a celebration in the open platz in front of the church during this visit, you may find a simple fruit cart parked there the next time you're in town. Be sure to always check to see what's new every time you're in this part of the world. Also, take plenty of photos and, when you have a moment, zoom in on each one to notice small details you may have missed during your visit.

MORE THAN JUST A PATHWAY

The stone pathway through the Garden Railway? It's not just a means to get a closer look at the trains and small villages, but  instead it represents a very popular tourism draw in Germany, The Romantic Road.

Leading from the town of Würzburg in central Germany to Füssen on the country's southern border, The Romantic Road stretches for 220 miles / 350 kilometres through quaint Bavarian towns and cities, such as Rothenburg ob der Tauber, Dinkelsbuhl, and Nordlingen, as well as past the picturesque castles of Harburg and Neuschwanstein, to provide travelers with an experience that is quintessentially German while revealing a wealth of European history, architecture, culture, and culinary delights. As you walk The Romantic Road at Epcot, note how the directional signs point to Füssen at one end, and back to Würzburg at the other.

ITALY

This next secret reveals again the Imagineers' commitment to detail and quality, even when it cannot be viewed up close by guests.

The Italy pavilion features a stunning replica of the historical bell tower of Saint Mark's Basilica in Venice, Italy, and high atop the campanile (the bell tower) is a beautiful golden statue of the Archangel Gabriel, painstakingly sculpted to match the original. Those guests wishing to get a closer look at this statue may view a nearly exact replica of this replica while touring the gardens within the Italy pavilion.

THE AMERICAN ADVENTURE

Every one of Walt Disney World's theme parks have what Walt called a "weenie", a prominent icon which beckons guests to draw closer. Most are readily apparent...in the Magic Kingdom it's Cinderella Castle, and in Disney's Animal Kingdom it's the Tree of Life.

Spaceship Earth is Epcot's "weenie", but there is also another weenie hidden by distance. Stand at Showcase Plaza and gaze across World Showcase Lagoon. There on the opposite shore standing proud is The American Adventure pavilion, the weenie for World Showcase.

Initially, Disney Imagineers thought of placing The American Adventure pavilion at the entrance to World Showcase as a way to convey that America was welcoming guests to the world. However, Dick Nunis, Disney's Chief of

Operations for all the parks, stated it should be on the far shore of World Showcase Lagoon so as to encourage guests to walk around the promenade. According to Marty Sklar, in his book, "Dream It! Do It!", Dick Nunis stated..."*We have to give our guests a key reason to go all the way around that big lagoon.*"..."*We need to put the big attraction - like the castle of the Magic Kingdom - at the far side of the lagoon to make people want to go there!*"

BETSY ROSS FLAG

Like the flags of Main Street, U.S.A., Liberty Square, and Frontierland, the flag flying atop the copula of the American Adventure pavilion adds to the story. Here, you see the "Betsy Ross" flag, which first flew in 1776, waving with a pattern of 13 stars in a circle, with each representing one of the original 13 colonies that fought for their independence during the Revolutionary War.

By the way, the American flag you see flying at the entrance to Epcot is a modern day flag displaying 50 stars.

AMERICA...STANDING TALLER THAN YOU THINK

Now take a moment to study another example of Disney's use of forced perspective. Standing in front of The American Adventure, you'll notice, by the placement and size of the doors and windows, that the building appears to be only two stories tall, which is because it reflects the design and architecture of Philadelphia's Independence Hall and Boston's Old State House. However, stand someone next to the building to give it proper scale and you'll discover it is actually 4 to 5 stories tall!

OWN A PIECE OF THE AMERICAN ADVENTURE

As with the wallpaper of the Haunted Mansion, the Disneyland Rose, the Mickey Mouse Plant or even the Asepso soap Hidden Mickey box, many guests enjoy owning a part of the Disney theme parks to have at home, and this next secret adds one more item to the list. Two, actually!

Take note of the scene in The American Adventure of the four men on the porch of the Depression era gas station. There on the wall, behind the banjo player, are two WPA era posters showcasing Great Smoky Mountains National Park and Fort Marion National Monument in St. Augustine, Florida. Both of these impressive posters are available for purchase through www.RangerDoug.com.

"Ranger Doug" is actually Doug Leen, a former seasonal Park Ranger who, in 1973 began leading the effort to rescue, restore and replicate the rare National Park posters which were produced under the WPA, beginning on August 26, 1938.

Note: The 1938 printing of the first of these posters by the WPA dates this porch scene to 1938 or later.

If you visit the Ranger Doug web site above, you'll find a very interesting history about these unique posters. *Photo courtesy of WDWGuidedTours.com.*

JAPAN

Stately in its presence, a five story pagoda welcomes guests to the Japan pavilion. Modeled after the 8th century Horyu-ji Temple in Nara, Japan, its architecture is more than simple form, function or design, but instead purposely represents a connection with the earth and heavens. Each of its five layers represent, in ascending order, Earth, Water, Fire, Wind and Heaven.

THE TIDES OF WORLD SHOWCASE LAGOON

This next secret is very subtle, yet adds a great deal to the story that is the Japan pavilion. Disney Imagineers, knowing World Showcase Lagoon is an enclosed body of water lacking tidal movement, added barnacles at the base of the large torii gate at the Japan waterfront to give guests a realistic impression of tidal movements in a salt-water environment.

ATTRACTING GOOD LUCK

Now turn from the torii gate and study the rooflines of the buildings in the Japan pavilion. Look carefully and you'll notice some are adorned with large golden fish. It is a belief in Japan that storks nesting on roofs bring good luck and happiness to the family inhabiting the building, so ornamental fish are often placed atop roofs to attract storks.

くす玉

Hanging from the small Garden House near the entrance to the Japan pavilion is a traditional Kusudama Ball. Though they are typically crafted today with brightly colored paper using the art of origami, the ball you see here reflects a more traditional style using aromatic greenery. So why is it here? A Kusudama Ball such as this is traditionally hung outside of restaurants and retail shops so as to bring good luck and prosperity.

MORE GOOD LUCK

In addition to the golden fish and Kusudama balls, bells large and small have long been a treasured tool to attract the attention of the gods and draw them near, where they will offer protection against evil. Study the rooflines of the pagoda at the entrance to the Japan pavilion, as well as other buildings, and notice the small intricately designed bells hanging from the corners of every level.

A CHERISHED CULTURAL ICON

While visiting the Japan pavilion, be sure to take a moment to discover a colorful cultural element that is highly respected throughout all of Japan...the Koi fish. Swimming in a small pond near the pavilion entrance, they are thought to bring good luck, prosperity and good fortune, as well as to embody perseverance, strength, courage, and beauty.

MICKEY'S HIDING WITH THE KOI

While viewing the Koi, look for the small silver grate in the water with a classic 3-circle Hidden Mickey on top.

WELCOME TO MOROCCO

Epcot's Morocco pavilion showcases the rich cultural heritage of Morocco, an African country known for its ancient history, the Moroccan desert, beautiful coastlines, and busy Medinas filled with colorful handcrafted goods. As you explore the pavilion,  you'll discover many features found today in the city of Fez, the country's religious and cultural center.

Entering the pavilion, you'll step into a courtyard with a beautifully painted 3-arch gate. This is actually an intricate replica of the Bab Boujouloud, the main gate into the ancient city of Fez. Step through the archways and enter a bustling medina, consisting of a labyrinth of narrow streets that wind their way past restaurants, palaces, fountains, and busy market stalls selling a vast collection of hand-crafted items, including jewelry, clothing, rugs, baskets, lamps, and more.

IT'S TIME FOR A SECRET

At first glance, it may appear to be simply an architectural decoration made up of 13 brass bowls, each perched on an ornate wooden corbel. However, it's much more than that. What you see high on a wall in the Morocco pavilion is a replica of the  Clock of the Abu Inania Medersa. Originally built on the façade of the Dar-Magana, or "House of the Clock", in Fez in 1357, this complicated clock doesn't operate with the gears, springs, and pendulums you would find in more modern clocks, but is instead "powered" and operated by water.

NEJJARINE FOUNTAIN

Step toward the back of the pavilion and there you will find a large ornately tiled fountain. Surrounded by planters, it's a pleasant feature of the pavilion, one which guests periodically stop at to photograph. This is, in fact, a replica of Fez's Nejjarine Fountain, which is found today in a busy market located in an older part town, the Fez el Bali, where it is frequented often as a popular source of water.

LOOK FOR ALADDIN

A stop at the Morocco pavilion can sometimes reveal one of children's favorite Disney characters. Journey far into the back of the pavilion, turn a corner and step inside a doorway adorned with a Mickey Mouse hand to look for Aladdin, who sometimes "flies" in on his carpet to greet guests, sign autograph books, and have a picture taken.

Note: Study the mural of the street scene backdrop and you'll find a Hidden Mickey! Hint: It's on the right side of the street.

THEY PROTECT AGAINST EVIL

As you journey through Morocco, you'll occasionally see what is called a Khamsa hand displayed on a door or wall, or as part of a decoration, or perhaps incorporated within a piece of jewelry. The Khamsa is an ancient symbol used throughout the Middle East and North Africa, and it is used as protection from bad luck, evil, and other dangers.

DON'T MISS
MORE MOROCCO

Many of the secrets at Walt Disney World are passed by because guests assume there's nothing to see there or they aren't welcome to explore. The Gallery of Arts and History at the Morocco pavilion is one such place. Hiding in plain sight, the façade gives the impression that it's all for decoration, so there is no sense in stopping here, but go ahead and open the two large doors to discover an ever-changing exhibit which showcases one of the many fascinating aspects of Morocco. See displays on the cultural apparel and accessories of Morocco that have been worn through the ages, learn about the challenges faced by the teams in the Rally of the Gazelles, an all woman desert rally, explore the world of the Berbers, the original inhabitants of the Sahara, or so much more. Go ahead and open the doors.

www.Disney-Secrets.com

A CLASSIC HIDDEN MICKEY

Out front, at the Sauk-Al-Magreb Gifts of Morocco, guests will find one of Epcot's most notable Hidden Mickeys. Take a moment to study the marketplace on the Showcase Lagoon side of the Morocco pavilion and find three plates arranged in a classic Hidden Mickey design. They may be moved periodically and change in appearance from time to time, but they're always there.

FRANCE

Here's an international example of the Imagineers' use of forced perspective.

As an iconic image of France, Disney Imagineers had no choice but to include the Eiffel Tower as part of the France pavilion, but they were faced with a bit of a problem. The Eiffel Tower's overwhelming size obviously would not fit *within* the pavilion, so they planned to construct a replica of the tower that was one-tenth the size of the original. However, they realized that guests viewing this replica up close would simply consider it to be an oversized model, so to solve this problem and to give the tower a sense of majestic height and distance, the Imagineers used forced perspective from top to bottom and placed the Eiffel Tower such that guests could not see its base. This creates the illusion the tower is as large as the original and approximately one mile away.

CE N'EST PAS VRAI

You'll often read that the Eiffel Tower of Epcot's France pavilion was built as an *exact duplicate* of Paris' tower using Gustave Eiffel's original blueprints, though scaled down to 1/10th the size. It's a good story, but if you compare photos of the two towers side by side, you'll realize that it's not true, since the original tower in Paris (Photo) contains far more iron work and architectural features.

PLUS QUE NE DISCERNE L'OEIL

Step inside the building for Souvenirs de France and Les Halles Boulangerie-Patisserie and take note of how it consists of two market halls, with one offering "dry goods" and the other nourishing French pastries. One might assume that this is simply a

pastry shop attached to a souvenir shop, but it is much more than that. From the two types of businesses and their close proximity to each other, to the architectural design and the iron trusses used overhead, this is a nod to the former Les Halles in Paris. In 1183, Philip Augustus built two market halls, or "halles", on the outskirts of Paris to offer textiles and other goods for sale to Parisians and travelers alike. In time, these halles bustled with shoppers and became the largest in the city. A couple hundred years later, food stalls were added to the market and soon Les Halles became known far and wide for its variety of fresh food, as well as its abundant selection of dry goods.

While here, take note of the sign on the wall that touts the services of the Souvenirs de France and Les Halles Boulangerie-Pattiserie, reading *Everything the Modern Parisian Needs* and *Nourishes the City of Lights Since 1183.*

LES HIDDEN MICKEY'S DE FRANCE

Pause and study the scrollwork near the sign for Les Vins de France and you'll discover an elaborate French Hidden Mickey.

FRENCH ATTENTION TO DETAIL

As you leave the France pavilion and head over the bridge to the United Kingdom, take a moment to move from the crowd and peer over both sides of the bridge railings to find more examples of the Disney Imagineers' attention to detail and storytelling.

www.Disney-Secrets.com

Bouquinistes Along the Seine River

Ahhhh, an afternoon in Paris...strolling through the Luxembourg Gardens, enjoying lunch at an outdoor café, choosing macaroons from a small patisserie, and perusing the wares of the Bouquinistes along the Seine to discover a vintage treasure or two.

Resting on the stone wall above the Seine river (World Showcase Lagoon) is a large green metal box opened to display a collection of antique French books, posters, and other artwork. Looking exactly like what you'd find in Paris, this "box" represents the Bouquinistes, a collection of booksellers who have lined both banks of the Seine river near Notre Dame with boxes similar to the one you see here, all of which offer for sale to passers by second-hand and antique books, a Parisian tradition that reaches back to the mid-1500s.

A rare first edition post-WWII issue of
Le Journal de Mickey –
Author's personal collection

www.Disney-Secrets.com

A View "Across the Pond"

Want to know one of the best places in this part of the world to watch the evening's fireworks? It's from the Terrace de Fleurs, between the France and UK pavilions. Get there early, as seating is somewhat limited.

United Kingdom

The largest secret at the United Kingdom pavilion literally surrounds guests as they walk its streets. Each of the buildings' facades and interiors represent a period of time, beginning with The Tea Caddy and its thatched roof representing the 1500s. The Queen's Table, the two-story building with diamond shaped wooden moldings, clovers and chevrons, denotes the 1600s, while its Queen Anne Room represents the 1700s, and the Lords and Ladies façade captures the architecture of the 1800s.

A Cantilevered Secret

Now take a moment to study the architecture near The Queen's Table. Notice how each ascending story is cantilevered above the previous story? In the period these buildings represent, taxes assessed on a building were based upon the square footage of the first floor. As a result, building owners sought to minimize the tax they owed by constructing buildings with a first floor having a narrow and small footprint, while ensuing floors were built larger and overhanging the first.

A Sporty Hidden Mickey

The large sign hanging above the entrance to the Sportsman's Shoppe holds a clever Hidden Mickey. Can you find it?

Revealed Only After Sunset

Some of the secrets you'll find at Walt Disney World are dependent upon the time of day. This next secret is truly unique, but it appears only after the sun sets, so if you pass by during the day, you'll have no idea it even exists. Make your way just beyond the Tea Caddy, as if you were heading over to the France pavilion, and there you will find a garden arbor arching over a pathway, with its underside lit by hundreds of tiny glowing lights creating a magical moment perfect for a picture.

A Touch of Old England

Standing to one side of the United Kingdom pavilion is a red pillar post box. Installed in countries wherever the British Empire ruled, it's a postal tradition with a history reaching back over 150 years. So how old is the box you see here? The answer lies in its "Royal Cypher", which is displayed on its front, at the base. Bearing the crown and royal cypher for Queen Elizabeth II,

this means it was installed here sometime after her reign began in February of 1952. The fanciful "R" of the royal cypher refers to "Regina", which is Latin for "Queen" and the letter "E" is in reference to Elizabeth, thus Queen Elizabeth. This post box is similar to the one you'll find in Harambe at Disney's Animal Kingdom, though it bears a royal cypher of "GIvR" for King George IV, who ruled until 1952, when Queen Elizabeth took the throne.

A DIGNIFIED SECRET

On the entrance sign to the Rose & Crown pub, you'll find the Latin phrase, "Otium cum Dignitate". Is it the royal dictate of a notable king? The battle cry of a decorated General? Perhaps the motto of oppressed servants? Actually, none of the above. It means simply *"Leisure with Dignity."* Fittingly adorning a pub, it refers to leisurely pursuits in retirement after a life of hard work.

LEISURELY ENJOYING THE VIEW

"Leisure with Dignity" is practiced with this next secret. Instead of walking past the UK Pavilion, step behind The Tea Caddy to find a collection of benches tucked amongst a colorful perennial garden designed to attract butterflies.

TEA FOR TWO...TOURS

It may appear to be just a beautiful garden behind The Tea Caddy, but it actually features plants that play a role in creating some of the finest tea blends of the world. What's the best way to learn about this horticultural secret? Every year, during the *Epcot International Flower and Garden Festival*, Twinings Tea at the UK pavilion offers two fascinating (for adults) tours which reveal the history of this very English drink, as well as the Twinings of London tea company. To sign up for either tour, visit The Tea Caddy Shop in the UK pavilion shortly after Epcot opens. There's no need for your entire party to sign up at once, and each tour hosts 20 guests. You may also call 407-WDW-Tour to make your reservations.

Royal Tea Garden Tour – A 45 minute guided tour where you'll enjoy a sampling of tea and scones. - $20 Per guest, tax included.

English Tea Garden Tour – Discover the history and art of tea blending in The Tea Caddy's elegant English Tea Garden. – Free – Same day signups are available in The Tea Caddy.

CANADA

The Canada pavilion employs two excellent examples of forced perspective. The Rocky Mountains above Victoria Gardens and the stately five-story Hotel du Canada are each designed to appear much higher than they actually are. Study the Hotel du Canada and take note of how the lowest windows are much larger than those at the base of its steeply pitched Mansard roof.

AN INSPIRING SECRET

With their finely manicured grounds and colorful blossoms, Canada's "Victoria Gardens" are inspired by the world-famous Butchart Gardens near Victoria, British Columbia.

A CANADIAN HIDDEN MICKEY

As you reach the top of the stairs at the entrance to the Canada pavilion, look for the large Totem Pole to the left. Study it carefully, and you'll discover a classic 3-Circle Hidden Mickey.

A WDW Guided Tours Tip:

If you're looking for a place to sit down for a quick "air conditioned" break on a hot day, head to the lobby of Reflections of China or the American Adventure to find a comfortable spot to sit and relax.

Courtesy of WDWGuidedTours.com

www.Disney-Secrets.com

SECRETS OF DISNEY'S HOLLYWOOD STUDIOS

"The World you have entered was created by The Walt Disney Company and is dedicated to Hollywood – not a place on the map, but a state of mind that exists wherever people dream and wonder and imagine, a place where illusion and reality are fused by technological magic. We welcome you to a Hollywood that never was – and always will be."

- Michael Eisner - Disney's Hollywood Studios Dedication

SID'S ONE-OF-A-KIND HIDDEN MICKEY

Step up onto the porch of Sid Cahuenga's One-Of-A-Kind Antiques and Curios after you enter Disney's Hollywood Studios and find your first Hidden Mickey of the day. Need a hint? Ask the Dalmatian.

CHEAP GAS AT OSCAR'S

Check the pumps over at Oscar's Super Station and you'll find the Disney Imagineers have priced gas at the same price you would have paid during the 1940s, the same era in which Oscar's is set...$0.19 cents per gallon!

STOP – THEN GO!

Before you begin to stroll down Hollywood Boulevard into Disney's Hollywood Studios, stop for a moment and watch the semaphore style traffic signal on the corner of Hollywood Blvd. and Prospect Ave. More than just a working decoration, this an exact duplicate of the type of traffic signals found in Los Angeles when Walt arrived in 1923. You'll find five such signals throughout Disney's Hollywood Studios, which is the same number of signals that Los Angeles first installed in 1920.

KEEPING YOU IN STITCHES

Here's a secret that gives a personal touch to your own souvenir. Visit Adrian & Edith's Head to Toe on Hollywood Blvd. and, for a price of usually $10 or less, have any Disney-Parks purchased item, such as shirts, caps, mouse ears, t-shirts, etc. embroidered with your own custom name, phrase or favorite Disney character.

EDDIE VALIANT

Located above the Hollywood & Vine restaurant are the offices of Eddie Valiant, Private Investigator. This is a nod to the character of Eddie Valiant, portrayed by actor Bob Hoskins in the 1988 Disney film *Who Framed Roger Rabbit*. Notice the year 1928 at the top of the building façade? That's a direct reference to the release of Steamboat Willie and Mickey Mouse's birthday, November 18, 1928.

MIND YOUR "PEAS" AND QS

If you choose to dine at the 50's Prime Time Café, (and I recommend you do) then you better be on your best behavior. Throughout their meals, diners are reminded to keep their elbows off the table, eat all of their vegetables, and to finish their homework before watching TV, all with some good-natured ribbing in an authentic 1950s atmosphere.

"They've Got a Tank!"

Step through the Indiana Jones Adventure Outpost and you'll spot a large tank set among German munitions and supplies. More than just a prop, this is the actual tank used in the 1989 film *Indiana Jones and the Last Crusade.*

Min and Bill's

Found on the west shore of Echo Lake is the *S.S. Down the Hatch*, an old tramp steamer that houses Min and Bill's Dockside Diner. *Min and Bill* was the name of a 1930 movie starring Marie Dressler (Min) and Wallace Beery (Bill), and it told the story of the struggles of Min, the manager of a run down dockside inn who raises a young woman, Nancy, to be a lady amidst the seedy and rough life of the docks, all while tangling with Bill, a loveable yet cantankerous fisherman. The film was a nationwide hit, earning Marie Dressler an Academy Award for Best Actress and propelling both her and Wallace Berry to stardom, with Berry eventually becoming MGM's highest paid actor in the early 1930s.

Flying high above Min and Bill's Dockside Diner is a set of International code flags and pennants, which borrows from a scene late in the movie. Flags such as these are used as a means to communicate between ships, and in this case, they communicate a nautical advertisement for sea-going sailors. Alternating between letters (flags) and numbers (pennants), the message spelled out between the two masts reads...

DOCKSIDE DINER
782562896354

While the meaning of the message "Dockside Diner" is apparent, the number sequence 782562896354 is a bit of an ongoing mystery. Given Disney Imagineers rarely place story elements in the park with no meaning, there is likely a hidden message in  these numbers. Perhaps they are the birthdates of the Imagineers who worked on the attraction? Research continues on this.

Note: The roman numerals "XXI" at the waterline of the stern reflects the draft of the ship. As you can see, the ship *appears* to be sitting nearly 21' deep in the water. *Photo courtesy of WDWGuidedTours.com*

SECRETS SCHEDULED TO SHIP

Standing in front of the Dockside Diner, you'll spot a couple of large wooden cargo containers all ready to be loaded aboard the ship. Reading the address stenciled on the side of one of the containers, you'll see it's destined for Mr. George Bailey  of Bedford Falls, which is a nod to the classic 1946 Christmas film *It's a Wonderful Life*, starring Jimmy Stewart. The other is a container of wine and spirits scheduled to arrive soon at Rick's Café Américain in Casablanca, Morocco. Here, it'll be signed for by Rick Blaine, who was played by Humphrey Bogart in the Academy Award winning 1942 film *Casablanca*.

GERTIE THE DINOSAUR

Located on the opposite shore of Echo Lake is Dinosaur Gertie's Ice Cream of Extinction. More than just a nod to the "California Crazy" novelty architecture of Los Angeles in the early 20th century, this towering dinosaur is Disney's homage to Winsor McCay, an American cartoonist who played a role in inspiring a young Walt Disney to become an animator. On February 18th, 1914, when Walt Disney was only 12 years old, Mr. McCay released an innovative silent cartoon titled *Gertie the Dinosaur*, which is recognized as being the very first cartoon ever produced to feature an animated character. Mr. McCay was also known for creating the comic strip series *Little Nemo* and *Dream of the Rarebit Fiend*, among others, as well as inventing (though not patenting) the Mutoscope, a popular form of entertainment during the turn of the 20th century and a precursor to animated cartoons and films.

As you approach Gertie by her tail, notice her footprints in the cement and the grass. Take note of how the Imagineers went to the extra effort of "cracking" the cement near her footprints to reflect her tremendous weight.

OFFICE SPACE FOR RENT

Make your way over to Peevy's Polar Pipeline, and you'll spot a sign in the window above that reads *Office Space for Rent.* Directly below the sign is a door that reads *Holly Vermont Realty – Hollywood – Beverly Hills.* If you're a fan of Walt Disney  and his inspiring history, then you'll appreciate the story behind this door.

In 1923, Walt arrived in Los Angeles with a suitcase full of his dreams, an abundance of ambition, only $40 in his pocket, and the hope for a fresh new start after experiencing the sharp sting of failure. Mickey Mouse had yet come to mind, but he was soon to sign a contract with Margaret Winkler to create an animated / real-life film series called *The Alice Comedies*, in which a live young girl sets off on adventures within a cartoon world with an animated cat named Julius. To make this happen, Walt needed some office space, and he found it in the back of the Holly Vermont Realty office at 4451 Kingswell Ave., which rented him an office for $10 a month. It was here that Walt and his brother, Roy, produced their new series, a creative success that provided the momentum for them to grow their business to ultimately become The Walt Disney Company.

You'll Impress 'Em

To the other side of Peevy's Polar Pipeline, just around the corner, you'll find a door for *Sights and Sound Acting and Voice Lessons.* In a bit of whimsy, read the three names on the door...

Ewell M. Pressem - Master Thespian
Singer B. Flatt - Voice Coach
Bill Moore - Account Executive

The Hollywood Brown Derby

The restaurant's name? It was coined in 1926 when Herbert K. Somborn opened what was initially a coffee shop in Los Angeles. At the time, the Governor of New York, Al Smith, was known for wearing his signature brown derby hat. He was in town when Herbert Somborn was choosing a name for his restaurant, so Herbert named it after the Governor's. . .brown derby.

The Stars Sign and Dine

Inside, directly across from the entrance to the Hollywood Brown Derby, is a large book in a glass case that holds the signatures of the many famous stars who have dined at Disney's Hollywood Studio's

200

Brown Derby restaurant. Note that the book is out on display only during operating hours.

DINE WITH A DISNEY IMAGINEER

Any guest can enjoy a wonderful meal at The Hollywood Brown Derby, but did you know you can also share a meal with a real Disney Imagineer here? You and up to nine other guests can reserve your own special meal where you'll dine with a Disney Imagineer while enjoying a four-course meal of contemporary American cuisine, all topped with amazing insights into the world of Disney Imagineering.

Dining with Disney Imagineers is available for lunch at The Hollywood Brown Derby and dinner at Citrico's restaurant in Disney's Grand Floridian Resort & Spa.

Tip: It is strongly recommended that you make reservations 180 days in advance. Call 407-WDW-DINE (407-939-3463) for additional information and to make those reservations.

"YOU'RE AN ORIGINAL, KID."

One of the first things you'll notice as you enter the Hollywood Brown Derby is the countless caricature drawings of famous stars that cover the walls. Note that the smaller drawings within the black frames are copies, while the larger drawings in the gold frames are all originals.

ANIMATION COURTYARD

At the entrance to the Animation Courtyard, you'll find three portals, with the two on each side displaying beautiful artwork depicting iconic moments in the world of movie-making. Make your way to the portal on the right and study the artwork until you find two animators drawing Goofy and Donald Duck.

VOYAGE OF A HIDDEN MICKEY

After stepping through the entrance portals into the Animation Courtyard, take a look at the sign for Voyage of the Little Mermaid to the left. If you study the bubbles in the water background, you'll find a classic three-circle Hidden Mickey.

R2D2 FOR $25K

Make your way into the Star Wars Launch Bay for a Star Wars souvenir that is out of this world. There, tucked into a corner, is a *full-sized* R2D2 droid for sale for only $25,000. Batteries not included.

MICKEY & MINNIE LIVE!

After sunset, make your way over to *Mickey & Minnie's Runaway Railway* and, using your iPhone, take a "Live" photo of the large flashing neon sign at the entrance. Then set the photo to "Loop" to watch this colorful sign come to life whenever and wherever you want.

RUNAWAY HIDDEN MICKEYS

Mickey & Minnie's Runaway Railway is an exciting adventure where *you* become part of the cartoon, traveling along with Mickey and Minnie Mouse, with Goofy as your locomotive engineer. Also accompanying you for the ride are quite a few Hidden

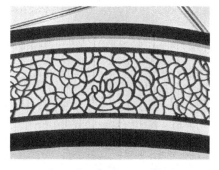

Mickeys. In fact, you'll be hard pressed to find them all as you make your way down the tracks, but keep an eye out for them in the lights of the queue, the background artwork, in the colorful fireworks, and even a reference to the year 1928 as you pass into a tunnel.

WORLD FAMOUS HANDPRINTS

Outside the entrance to Mickey & Minnie's Runaway Railway, you'll find the handprints and signatures of famous celebrities, including a couple of world famous mice!

THE HISTORY OF WALT

Showcasing the life of Walt Disney, from growing up in small-town America to introducing the world to Mickey Mouse and the stories of Disneyland, Walt Disney Presents is one of my favorite attractions in all of Walt Disney World. Here, guests can see the very desk that Walt sat at and carved his initials into while in 2nd grade...when you could carry a pocket knife to school, the actual Abraham Lincoln Audio-Animatronic that stunned the world at the 1964 – 1965 New York Worlds Fair, the intricate "Granny's House" that Walt himself constructed in miniature using a scene from his 1949 film *So Dear to My Heart*, intricate models of Disneyland's Sleeping Beauty Castle and Jungle Cruise, and much, much more. If you're a fan of Walt Disney and Disney history, then you'll want to be sure to step off the well worn path to the thrill-ride attractions and make your way inside.

MICKEY & MINNIE
SAVE THE DAY!

While walking through Walt Disney Presents, you may have noticed a small vintage Mickey Mouse Hand Car toy in a display case. It's a cute toy, to be sure, but to The Lionel Corporation, it is much, much more than that.

In the late 1920s, electric Lionel model trains were very popular with parents and children around the world, especially during Christmastime. However, the Great Depression of 1929 brought sales of such "luxury" items to a halt, as millions of people throughout America and around the world suddenly found themselves out of work. With their customers now unable to afford Lionel trains, the company found itself facing the prospect of bankruptcy by May of 1934.

In July of that same year, Walt's merchandising genius, Kay Kaymen, approached The Lionel Corporation with the idea of working together to create a new toy featuring Mickey & Minnie Mouse, and the result of that collaboration is the Mickey & Minnie Hand Car you see here. Priced at only $1, and featuring two of the biggest stars in the world at that time, the toy was an instant and wildly popular hit, selling over a quarter million hand cars within only four months, thus ultimately saving The Lionel Corporation. *Photo courtesy of the Walt Disney Family Museum*

THE "DANCING MAN"
PROTOTYPE FIGURE

Be it a towering fire-breathing dragon in Fantasmic! at Disneyland, a menacing yeti high on Mt. Everest, or a collection of jailed pirates trying to coax a set of keys from an unwilling dog in Pirates of the Caribbean, Disney's Audio-Animatronics have always played a key role in telling the story within some of guests' favorite attractions.

As you move along in Walt Disney Presents, you'll come upon a tiny man standing on a small wooden stage. Compared to what you might find over on Batuu or perhaps Pandora, this vintage story element doesn't appear to be that impressive, but this small  "Dancing Man", now over 70 years old, *is the very precursor to all of the advanced Audio-Animatronics you see in use at Disney theme parks around the world today.*

Note: Walt had an interest in building miniatures, and he was quite skilled at it. With the design help from animator Ken Anderson, he built by hand the very opera house stage you see here, as well as the nearby "Granny's Cabin".

A SEMINAL MOMENT
IN DISNEY HISTORY

 When Walt was asked to develop four different attractions for the 1964 – 1965 World's Fair in New York, he realized he had been presented with an opportunity to develop and enhance exciting new technologies that he had been working on which could be showcased to the world... before being returned for use at Disneyland. One of these was the Great Moments with Mr. Lincoln attraction for the State of Illinois pavilion. Building upon the results of the "Dancing Man", as well as the cutting-edge Audio-Animatronic advances he had created for the Enchanted Tiki Room at Disneyland, Walt set

out to invent and present the first Audio-Animatronic human in the form of our 16th President, Abraham Lincoln. Rising up from his chair to deliver dramatic speeches on freedom, liberty, and civil rights, the resulting figure was so lifelike and impressive, that it captivated the world's attention, as this was the first time anyone had ever seen anything like it.

The Audio-Animatronic Abraham Lincoln figure you see within the Walt Disney Presents attraction is not a recreation, but instead the very same Abraham Lincoln figure that rose from his chair at the 1964 – 1965 New York World's Fair and amazed the world.

UNLOCK THIS MUPPET SECRET

As you enter the Muppet-Vision 3D attraction, you'll find a fun secret that is missed by thousands of guests every day. Just as you pass through the turnstiles, look to your right and you'll find a sign hanging in the window which reads, "Back in 5 Minutes. *Key is under Mat.*" Go ahead and lift the mat!

MUPPET VISION 3D WORLD HEADQUARTERS DIRECTORY

As you enter the Muppet Vision 3D attraction, look for the building directory to your left. Here, you'll find, amongst others...

INSTITUTE OF HECKLING & BROWBEATING
Statler and Waldorf – Curmudgeons in Chief – Box A Mezz

MUPPET KITCHENS & PYROTECHNIC RESEARCH
Swedish Chef – Tippy Top Cookie Guy – Suite 264

SARTORIAL ACCUMULATION DIVISION
Miss Piggy – Diva – Very Suite 4444

ACADEMY OF AMPHIBIAN SCIENCE
Kermit The Frog – Suite 5235

DIVISION OF DECIEBEL DEVELOPMENT
Animal – Percussionist at Large – Suite 6420

AN HOMAGE TO
A FAMOUS MOUSKETEER

The next Walt Disney World secret is more for mom and dad. As you enter the staging area for the Muppet Vision 3-D attraction, you'll notice "a net full of Jell-O" hanging from the ceiling on the left and toward the back. Ponder this, and you'll realize this is a nod to Annette Funicello, perhaps the most famous of all Mouseketeers.

PIPE DOWN, GONZO

The Muppet Vision 3-D attraction is filled with all kinds of quirky signs and messages inside and out. To the right of the entrance, following the queue line, find the large pipe turned downward and you will have found the Imagineers' playful tribute to Gonzo the Great. Of course, the pipe represents Gonzo's nose!

CATCH GONZO IN TIME

This next secret is for those who are looking down at their phones or are unaware of their surroundings. Did you catch the time as you entered the Muppet Vision 3-D attraction? If not, don't worry, Gonzo did. Take a look at the large clock at the entrance to the attraction and spot Gonzo hanging from the minute hand. In case you're wondering, he'll go around the clock face 8,760 times in the next year!

A HIDDEN MICKEY
ICE CREAM BAR

While visiting the Stage 1 Company Store, where you'll find plenty of "Muppet Stuff", make your way over to the paint cans and find yourself a Hidden Mickey of a different kind. This one is of a Mickey Mouse Ice Cream Bar!

IT'S READY FOR IT'S CLOSE UP

The large colorful Hollywood stage backdrop against the wall inside the Stage 1 Company Store? It's an *actual* backdrop from the television program, *The Muppet Show.*

ANOTHER SPILLED HIDDEN MICKEY?!

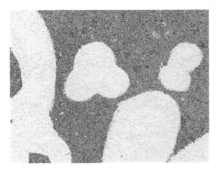

As you make your way around the exterior of the Stage 1 Company Store, watch where you step, as there is a lot of spilled paint. One of those spills, however, formed another spilled Hidden Mickey!

BACKLOT EXPRESS HIDDEN MICKEY

If it's time for something to eat, then it's time to discover a Hidden Mickey. Visit Backlot Express and find a large pillar near the hot coffee and cocoa machines. There, on its side, is a bit of a mess of paint that makes up a 3-circle Hidden Mickey.

YOU WEREN'T SUPPOSED TO SEE THAT

From the entrance door at Club 33 and attraction refurbishment walls, to landscaping features and even entire backstage buildings, you've heard about Disney's magical paint color known by such names as "Go Away

Green", "No-See-Um-Green", or "Green Away", but have you ever seen a can of it? Well, here's your chance. While you're in Backlot Express, find the shelf of paint cans and you'll discover this mythical color of Disney legend and lore.

SUNSET BOULEVARD

Most guests to Disney's Hollywood Studios step right on top of this next secret and never even realize it. Others stare right at it, but haven't a clue as to its significance.

On the street corners of Sunset Boulevard, guests will find an imprint in the cement which reads, *Mortimer & Co. 1928 Contractors*. This is an homage to Mortimer Mouse, the name Walt Disney originally considered for Mickey Mouse, and 1928 is a reference to the year in which Mickey Mouse was not only "born", but also made his debut in the animated cartoon *Steamboat Willie*.

Note: The image you see here is an optical illusion for most viewers. While the letters appear raised, they're actually imprinted into the concrete so they won't wear away with all of the guest foot traffic. To view the image properly, think of the light source as coming from the lower left corner, instead of the upper right.

A TRIBUTE TO FLORA DISNEY?

This next secret is a bit of a mystery. It is a tribute, but to whom?

Located in the ticket booth of the Legends of Hollywood Theater on Sunset Blvd. is an antique paperweight. With a date of 1958 being clearly visible on the left of two medallions, the paperweight commemorates the 50th anniversary of New York's stately Singer Building, which was built in 1908 and, for a brief period, was the tallest building in the world. Measuring 4.5

inches long and 2.5 inches wide, the paperweight is made of bronze, and the handle itself is an exact replica of the small bronze anchors which the window cleaners used when anchoring themselves to the exterior of the building.

Nothing in the parks is placed at random by the Imagineers, especially a piece such as this. The small sign on the General Store in Frontierland for A.C. Dietz Lanterns ties to Walt and the early days of Disneyland, the gas lamps of Main Street, U.S.A. are exact replicas of the very first gas street lamp ever used in America, and the colorful Mutoscopes of Town Square are an obscure tribute to Winsor McCay, whom is recognized by Disney as being a very important inspiration for Walt becoming an animator.

Initially, one might think this is an obvious tribute to Isaac Merritt Singer, the inventor of the Singer Sewing Machine, but he lived well before Walt's time and had no interactions with Walt. In addition, while the Singer Building was located in New York, it was not home to the offices of Charles Mintz, the man who stole Oswald the Lucky Rabbit from Walt, or Margaret Winkler, the woman who helped Walt a great deal. Both would make for a perfect tie in with the paperweight's placement in the theater, but they have no application here.

It turns out this paperweight may be a cleverly hidden tribute to Walt's mother, Flora. In 1906, Walt's parents, Elias and Flora, moved their family to Marceline, Missouri. Shortly after their arrival, Elias bought Flora a sewing machine, and given Singer sewing machines were by far the most popular model in use across the country at the time, it is safe to assume it was a Singer model. In my research involving the Walt Disney Hometown Museum, they indicated that Walt's sister, Ruth, had told the Museum's Director that Flora was an accomplished seamstress, making clothing for the entire family. In addition, she was also part of a rural farm organization that made quilts in the area.

But why is this tribute located in the Legends of Hollywood Theater? It may be because Isaac Singer was at one time a theater manager in New York before going on to invent the Singer Sewing Machine Flora Disney would use to clothe Walt and the entire Disney family throughout the years, beginning in Marceline. *Photo courtesy of WDWGuidedTours.com*

SECOND ASSISTANT DIRECTORS DO THE HEAVY LIFTING

On a second story window above a shop on Sunset Blvd., you'll see a reference to the *International Brotherhood of Second Assistant Directors*, or the IBSAD. Next to this is a window for the *Muscle Beach Bodyguard Service*. These two windows are a nod to those individuals in the film industry with the title and job responsibilities of Second Assistant Director. In this valued role, they take care of all of the *heavy lifting* required to keep a film on schedule and on budget, all while *protecting* the backside of the First Assistant Director; they monitor the whereabouts of the cast and manage their time so that they are on set, on time, and ready to act when required, communicate important information to the cast and crew, obtain "extras" for filming, handle communications between varied departments, update decision makers on the day's status, as well as countless other tasks. Their go-go-go job requires endurance, which is why the Imagineers have placed a stationary bike behind the IBSAD window!

SUNSET CLUB
HIDDEN MICKEYS

Art Deco meets Hidden Mickeys on the exterior of the Sunset Club Couture on Sunset Blvd. Look up and spot a Hidden Mickey in the art deco frieze at the roof line, as well as adorning the windows at street level.

BEAUTY AND THE BEAST
LEAVES AN IMPRESSION

If you opt not to see the *Beauty and The Beast - Live on Stage* performance, you will join the thousands who pass by this next secret each and every day unaware it exists. Make your way toward the entrance of the attraction and note all of the famous celebrities who have left their handprints, as well as carved their names, in the cement.

ROCK 'N' ROLLERCOASTER STARRING AEROSMITH

Walk this way through the Rock 'N' Rollercoaster Starring Aerosmith attraction to discover a fun collection of Hidden Mickeys.

As you make your way through the queue, you'll come to a section of flooring that is made up of colorful irregularly shaped tiles. Look for two small Hidden Mickeys here, each made up of three circles that definitely stand out amongst the tiles once they're discovered.

Next, search for a coiled cable Hidden Mickey on the floor when the band invites you to join along on the ride, as well as another hidden in the carpet. You're not done yet, however, as you'll also find one in the image of the band atop the limo, one

that you "pick", another that makes for a colorful and moving finish, and more. Remember, it's a *sweet emotion* when you find them before getting *back in the saddle again* to enjoy Disney's Hollywood Studios.

THE TWILIGHT ZONE TOWER OF TERROR

This next secret is an homage to a character in a classic episode of The Twilight Zone.

After entering the lobby of the Twilight Zone Tower of Terror, look for a pair of reading glasses sitting on the Concierge Desk. The glasses are a reference to the Twilight Zone episode "Time Enough at Last" in which Henry Bemis, (Portrayed by Burgess Meredith) a bookish man who loves to read, finds himself as the last man on  earth after an atomic blast. He's thrilled to discover the ruins of a library packed with all kinds of fascinating books, and now, being all alone on the planet, he finally has all the time he wants to read them. The cruel irony of the Twilight Zone strikes, however, when to his horror he accidentally drops his glasses and breaks the lenses.

Now notice the poster behind the Concierge Desk that reads, "Anthony Fremont and His Orchestra". This is a reference to what is considered by many to be the best Twilight Zone episode ever produced. In this episode, titled "It's a Good Life", a young Anthony Fremont (Bill Mumy) is a six-year old boy who controls the world with god-like mental powers, but unfortunately wields them with the unlimited restraint and mind of a child, thus filling everyone in his town with fear. In addition to being able to control the weather, read minds, think objects into being and cast away people he doesn't like, young Anthony Fremont likes music, but he doesn't like singing, hence the musically themed poster.

The landscaping outside the Hollywood Tower Hotel isn't just random growth. It was designed specifically to mimic the hillsides found around the Elysian and Griffith Parks areas of Los Angeles as a means to lend more authenticity to this Hollywood area hotel.

The music playing? It's Glenn Miller's "Sleepy Time Gal" and Duke Ellington's "Mood Indigo", two songs that were popular at the time the Hollywood Tower Hotel was struck by lightning on October 31, 1939.

In a nod to the Disney Imagineers' attention to detail, within the lobby of the Tower of Terror is a copy of the Los Angeles Examiner newspaper dated on Halloween night, October 31, 1939. Fittingly, the cover story is about the capture of Ruth Judd, who escaped from prison where she had been sentenced for murder.

"Ruth Judd Gives Self Up After Six Days,
Returns to Asylum in Hysterics"

Note: This same newspaper appears at the Disneyland, Disney's Hollywood Studios and Disneyland Paris Tower of Terror attractions.

TWILIGHT ZONE HIDDEN MICKEY

The Twilight Zone Tower of Terror is home to a number of Hidden Mickeys. Guests watching the episode of *The Twilight Zone* that introduces the attraction will notice a stuffed Mickey Mouse doll being held by a little girl as she and her family board the  elevator. In addition, as your elevator car reaches the "fifth dimension," pay special attention to the swirling stars and watch them quickly form the head of Mickey Mouse.

A Rerun for the First Time

Think you've seen that episode of *The Twilight Zone* before? Chances are you have...at least the initial portion of it. The Imagineers created this custom episode specifically for the attraction, and they drew inspiration for it from the opening moments of a 1961 episode titled *It's a Good Life*.

Tip: For a fun family photo when riding the Twilight Zone Tower of Terror, hold up your park map and act as if you're casually studying it just at the moment the elevator drops...and the camera flashes. While the photo captures those around you screaming in terror, you appear cool, calm and collected while searching the map for where to find a churro. Better yet, use a book for an even more casual look. Be sure to hold the map or book a bit low, or it will rise and obscure your face in the photo as the elevator drops!

Those Are Andy's Footprints

As you enter Toy Story Land, take note of the large footprints embedded into the concrete. These belong to Andy, and the reason they are so large is that when you entered Toy Story Land, you shrank and became the size of one of Andy's toys!

HIDDEN MICKEY MANIA!

As you prepare to board your tram and test your carnival shooting prowess on Toy Story Mania!, look for the large Hidden Mickey on a wall featuring Mr. Potato Head, Slinky Dog, and Bullseye.

THE PRICE FOR REX IS NOVEMBER 22, 1995

Over by the queue of the Slinky Dog Dash roller coaster attraction, just where Slinky begins his run, is an oversized box for Rex, the Tyrannosaurus Rex. Check the price sticker on the box and you'll see that its 11 22 coding and $19.95 price is a nod to the release date for the original *Toy Story* movie, November 22, 1995.

And as you leave the Toy Story Mania! attraction, take note of the

price sticker from Al's Toy Barn placed in the corner of the oversized box for the Lenny Wind-Up Toy Binoculars. The code of 11 13, combined with the price of $.99 makes up the release date of *Toy Story 2*, which is November 13, 1999.

THE MILLENNIUM FALCON IN MINIATURE

Believe it or not, but when you're looking at the Millennium Falcon, you're actually seeing double, it's just that the second Millennium Falcon is much, much smaller.

Tucked up underneath the underside of the larger Millennium Falcon, amongst all of the pipes and valves, is a small model of the same ship. Stand near the cockpit and look just below the band of grating that circles the cockpit. If you look immediately below the very base of the band you'll spot a small Millennium Falcon approximately 6 inches across clinging upside down to a section of the ship's underside.

THESE TIE IN, TOO

As with the miniature Millennium Falcon, a number of TIE Fighters can also be found scattered throughout the ship. Look for the half a dozen or so small panels of six "bolts" found at various places on the prominent band of tubes, hoses, manifolds, boxes, valves, coils, etc., which makes its way around the ship. Within each of these panels of six bolts, one of them is actually a small TIE fighter, according to the rebels of Batuu.

Fusion Generator Supply Tanks

As you smuggle goods through the corridors and pathways of Batuu while avoiding the attention of Storm Troopers, you'll no doubt notice the large light colored "cubes" scattered about. These are actually Fusion Generator Supply  Tanks. A nod to the 1977 film, *Star Wars: A New Hope*, you may recall seeing these at the homestead of Luke Skywalker's Uncle Owen on the planet Tatooine.

Track the Theming

As with Walt Disney World on the planet Earth, you'll find the pavement used throughout Star Wars: Galaxy's Edge contains creative elements which contribute to the Star Wars story. As you make your way about Battu East, look for the tracks of various animals,   as well as the tread marks of familiar droid units. Here, the Disney Imagineers took an impression of the tread pattern on R2D2 in the 1977 film *Star Wars: A New Hope* and used that very pattern to make the tracks you see winding their way along the pathway.

www.Disney-Secrets.com

TRASH TO SECTOR 3263827

In the 1977 film *Star Wars: A New Hope*, Luke, Han, Leia and Chewbacca become stranded in a massive trash "masher" located in Detention Block AA-23 of the Death Star. The hatch number of the trash compactor was 3263827, so it's only fitting that the trash cans found throughout Batuu each display this designation. I wonder if each one is also inhabited by a Dianoga?

IT'S A GOOD BET THE EMPIRE KNOWS YOU'RE HERE

As you make your way about Batuu, you'll come across a station where you can drop off your droid for repairs. You won't want to linger, however, since hanging in a net nearby is an Imperial Probe Droid, just like the one that notified the Empire of the rebel base on Planet Hoth. Though in a state of disrepair, you can never be too sure.

REMEMBER...YOU'RE ON BATUU

Having trouble locating something in Dok-Ondar's Den of Antiquities? Want to find the fastest way back to Sunset Blvd.?

Or maybe you'd like a photo taken of you using your phone. Then ask any one of the Cast Members for assistance. However, don't be surprised at their response. After all, this is Batuu.

YOUR EYES
WON'T DECEIVE YOU

"With the blast shield down, I can't even see. How am I supposed to fight?!" - Luke Skywalker

In the 1977 film, *A New Hope*, Luke Skywalker dons a helmet and lowers the blast shield to test his skills against a remote, and to learn to trust the Force. Look above the Holochess Table while aboard the Millennium Falcon and you'll notice the same helmet and remote sitting on a shelf, ready to train you in the ways of the Force.

PORG NESTS

As you wait in the queue and staging area for Millennium Falcon: Smugglers Run, take notice of the small "bird nest" like piles of wiring tucked into corners, amongst pipes, atop ledges, and elsewhere. These are porg nests, belonging to the small flat-muzzled avians that make their home on the rocky cliffsides of Luke Skywalker's secluded island.

THE BLACK SPIRE

Located outside the entrance to Dok-Ondar's Den of Antiquities is a towering rock spire. This is *the* Black Spire, the one for which this remote outpost is named. Here, you'll find a collection of famous and infamous traders, smugglers, merchants, and travelers of all kinds roaming the area, many of whom prefer not to be found.

DOK-ONDAR'S
DEN OF ANTIQUITIES

Step through the door of Dok-Ondar's Den of Antiquities and you'll discover not only Dok-Ondar himself in the back of the shop, but also an impressive collection of rare and unique items, which he has acquired from across the galaxy. Take a moment to study the second story of his shop and discover an abundance of items from all of the Star Wars movies, including a bust of Yoda, a large taxidermied Wampa...with both arms, a golden Jar Jar Binks, and more.

KEEP CLEAR OF THE SARLACC

In the 1983 film *Return of the Jedi*, Luke, Han, and Chewie were soon to meet their deadly fate at the hand of Jabba the Hutt and a large sarlacc waiting in the sands of the Great Pit of Carkoon. Luke offered Jabba one last chance to free the three of them or die, but he refused to take it, leading to Jabba's demise in an exciting scene where the heroes were victorious once again. Here is *your* chance to see a sarlacc in person. Step inside Dok-

Ondar's Den of Antiquities and find the sarlacc that Dok-Ondar has procured and put on display. Though small, it is still quite dangerous. Heed the warning in Aurebesh, which reads *Warning – Keep Clear of Beak and Tentacles.*

CARVED IN STONE

Catch it in the wrong light, and you won't notice that the large stone just outside of Dok-Ondar's Den of Antiquities has an image of Dok-Ondar carved into its surface.

www.Disney-Secrets.com

"SHUT DOWN ALL OF THE DRINKING FOUNTAINS ON THE DETENTION LEVEL!"

You may think twice about using the drinking fountain in Batuu. Press the button and enjoy a refreshing drink or refill your water bottle, but keep an eye out for another eye. Pushing the button on the drinking fountain alerts the creepy one-eyed Dianoga that you're there, and it may rise in the tank to get a look at whomever has dared to drain the murky water from the rusty pipes in which it lives.

In case you're wondering if the water is safe to drink, don't worry, as the message in Aurebesh on the front of the tank reads *Contamination threat level low.* Unfortunately, the line above it, in red, reads *Contamination threat level critical.* And to add a bit of clarity, the sign directly above the water fountain itself reads *WARNING – This water is not safe to consume for most life forms. Please drink with caution.*

Choose wisely.

A TRIBUTE TO THE TRILOGY

Found atop and inside Docking Bay 7 are large cargo pods with the numbers 77, 80, and 83 displayed on their sides. These are a nod to the years 1977, 1980, and 1983, the years in which the first Star Wars movies were released.

REMEMBERING MARDJI

This next secret is a tribute to a Star Wars actor which few, if any, guests ever notice. Up on a shelf in Docking Bay 7, somewhat out of the way, is a container with an image of a Bantha on the front. In Aurebesh it reads, *Blue Bantha - Imported from Tatooine - Home of Mardji.* This is the Disney Imagineers' touching tribute to Mardji, the Asian elephant that "portrayed" a Bantha in *Star Wars: Episode IV A New Hope.* With their massive size, long thick fur, and large horns, Banthas served as beasts of burden for Tusken Raiders on the planet of...you guessed it...Tatooine.

LOTH CAT

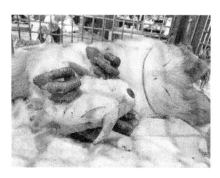

Visit Merchant Row and take notice of the Loth Cat sleeping in the cage in the middle of The Creature Stall. Watch for a moment and you'll notice it is slowly breathing as it peacefully dreams of chasing Loth Rats. Now take note of one of the cages suspended from the ceiling above. Look closely and you'll see a creature inside...and it's watching you. There are more about, some who are watching, and others that rustling inside their cage looking for a way to get out.

CLASSIC STAR WARS SCENES

Cross the street over to the Toydarian Toymaker shop and look up to find a handful of classic scenes depicted in a marionette-like form above. See Obiwan Kenobi battle Darth Vader, find the Millennium Falcon outwitting Tie Fighters, and imagine all of  the action as Luke, Han, Leia, and Chewbacca battle Jabba the Hutt at the Great Pit of Carkoon.

"NO ATTRACTION'S EVER REALLY GONE"

 Nearby, out in the marketplace, you'll find three landspeeders stacked one atop another on a rack. Take a look at the middle landspeeder and you'll note three Aurebesh characters on its battered side. The characters translate to L-M-A, and they are a clever nod by the Disney Imagineers to the former attraction that used to reside in this space, *Lights! Motors! Action! Extreme Stunt Show*. It's interesting to note that this same landspeeder at Batuu West (Disneyland) carries the same L-M-A designation, even though *Lights! Motors! Action! Extreme Stunt Show* never existed there.

CATCH OF THE DAY

Batuu is home to skilled smugglers, so it only makes sense that they can get pretty much whatever they'd like at the outpost, including fresh fish. Inside Oga's Cantina, you'll find the fish of the day packed in ice and stacked in crates. On the side of the crates, the Aurebesh reads *Frozen Fresh.*

TRILON WISHING TREE

Make your way to the courtyard of Savi's Workshop where you'll find a tree adorned with colorful strips of cloth tied to its branches. Here, Batuuans ask the galaxy to grant their wishes by tying a piece of cloth to the tree, and when it disintegrates and falls, their wish is granted.

Many thanks to Dave Drumheller of WDWGuidedTours.com for his keen eye in finding Star Wars Land secrets, as well as his superior Aurebesh translation skills. Thanks Dave!

www.Disney-Secrets.com

SECRETS OF DISNEY'S
ANIMAL KINGDOM

"Welcome to a kingdom of animals...real, ancient and imagined: a kingdom ruled by lions, dinosaurs and dragons: a kingdom of balance, harmony and survival; a kingdom we enter to share in the wonder, gaze at the beauty, thrill at the drama, and learn."

- Michael Eisner – Dedication of Disney's Animal Kingdom

AN EXCLUSIVE ENTRANCE

Next I reveal a secret side entrance to Disney's Animal Kingdom that will have you skirting long lines in the hot Florida sun.

Crowds at the entrance to Disney's Animal Kingdom can be quite large. While others wait in long lines at the main entrance, step over to the adjoining Rainforest Cafe and make your way toward the rear of the gift shop where you will find a separate out-of-the-way entrance to Disney's Animal Kingdom.

AN INTERACTIVE HELLO

Upon arriving at the park first thing in the morning, most guests rush to enter the Oasis and quickly move on to their favorite attractions, and it is here that they miss one of the first secrets of the day. Make it a point to arrive at Disney's Animal Kingdom early in the morning and you will find Cast Members standing nearby who are holding small sociable animals for up close interaction with children and other guests.

THE OASIS

As with all Disney parks, guests are taken on a journey of transition from the outside world to a land of magic and wonder as they enter Disney's Animal Kingdom.

As you move through The Oasis, refrain from rushing further into the park and take a moment to notice how the Disney Imagineers purposely designed it to transition guests from the outside world to the world of wonder that awaits. Notice how enchanting music has begun to fill the air while winding paths, cool waterfalls, towering plants, and lush greenery all begin to transport guests to another land. Just as with emerging from the tunnels into the Town Square at the Magic Kingdom, guests emerge from The Oasis to a stage of exotic animals, stunning habitats, exciting thrills and engaging education.

Tip: If you take the time to slowly stroll through The Oasis and explore its different paths, caves, foliage and waterfalls, you will discover the beautiful (and sometimes noisy) Macaws, each perched close to the trail. Of course, you'll also find many other birds roosting in  the trees or perhaps preening at the water's edge. However, be sure to gaze into the water, as well, as you'll no doubt spot some interesting fish, including the exotic Spotted Gar.

CURB APPEAL

 One of the first things you'll notice when entering Disney's Animal Kingdom is that, unlike the Magic Kingdom, Epcot, and Disney's Hollywood Studios, the "street curbs" here are undefined and blend into the jungle.

Follow the Right Path

After passing through the Oasis, you'll be greeted by the icon of the park, the Tree of Life. You're anxious to explore, so you'll be tempted to head left to Pandora or Africa, or right to Dinoland U.S.A. or Asia. Instead, take some time to discover the trails that wind their way to and around the base of the Tree of Life. Here, you can study up close the animals that make up the bark, enjoy a quiet path among the greenery, or maybe discover an ancient tortoise slowly making its way along.

A 30' Height Limit

As you walk past, in and around the buildings of Disney's Animal Kingdom, notice how they are often overshadowed by tall trees and objects. The Imagineers purposely limited the height of buildings in this park to 30 feet, thus capturing and conveying the dominating essence of the landscape.

The Tree of Life

Stop and pay attention to the leaves of The Tree of Life. Watch them for a while and you'll notice they're not static, but instead moving every time the wind blows. Note that because the Tree of Life is not real, it cannot grow leaves. As a result, the Imagineers had to affix each and every leaf on the tree, and to ensure it all looked realistic when finished, each leaf was designed to gently move in the breeze.

It's no secret that the Tree of Life is large. At 14-stories tall, it rises 145 feet high. Its bark is a tapestry of over 350 carved animals, and its 8,000 branch tips hold 103,000 leaves made up of five different shades of green.

A TRIBUTE TO JANE GOODALL

Near the entrance to It's Tough to be a Bug, you'll find a touching tribute to Jane Goodall, a British primatologist who engaged in courageous ground-breaking research of primates in the wild as part of her 45-year study of their social interactions in Gombe Stream National Park, Tanzania. The tribute consists of a plaque and an impressive sculpture of David Greybeard, a grey-chinned male chimpanzee who was the first to accept Jane Goodall into his community. The sculpture provides an excellent opportunity to see the detailed work of the Tree of Life bark up close.

CAN'T JOIN THE FOLD

Everyone loves a free souvenir. The Disney Imagineers discovered this in the early days of Disneyland, as it seems guests would sometimes take anything from the park that wasn't nailed down. With the 3-D glasses for

It's Tough to be a Bug! being somewhat small and obviously "mobile", they had to come up with a way that would keep guests from taking them home as a souvenir, otherwise they'd have to replace thousands of glasses every day. The trick?...they designed them such that they cannot be folded, thus making them more difficult to stow or walk away with.

HARAMBE

In designing the village of Harambe, which means "Let's work together.", the Imagineers borrowed from the architectural elements found in the coastal town of Lamu in Kenya and Arusha in Tanzania. Realizing the story reaches far beyond just the architecture, they incorporated the elements that make Harambe seem even more realistic, including the stucco exterior of the town's buildings and structures, its cracked sidewalks,  dusty pathways, distinctive signs, overhead power and telephone lines, the sounds of commotion, and more.

HARAMBE...DOWN TO THE SMALLEST OF DETAILS

Making your way into the queue for Festival of the Lion King, you'll spot on the wall a plaque declaring the building to be an "Official Harambe Heritage Site". Note the date cited here, as it is the opening day for Disney's Animal Kingdom, April 22, 1998.

Now notice the collection of 8 small screws used to affix the plaque to the wall. In the Imagineer's attention to the smallest of details, they used four different kinds of old screws here. They no doubt had access to countless screws that were not only brand new, but also all of the same design, yet they chose screws that appeared to have perhaps come from an old can of screws, nails, and bolts that had been collected over the years, which more accurately represents what would happen with construction in Harambe.

"WATT'S" THIS SECRET?

If you visit the Tusker House Restaurant and step inside the main door, you'll spot to your left, low on a wall, a black Type H WattHour Meter. Look closely at the four dials displayed and you'll notice they reflect the total number of kilowatts used to-

date as 1998, which is also a tribute to the year in which Disney's Animal Kingdom opened.

A TRIBUTE TO JOE RHODE

If it's time to eat, then it's time for discovering a secret that is a nod to Joe Rhode, the Disney Imagineer who played the lead role in designing and developing Disney's Animal Kingdom. Step inside Tusker House Restaurant and look up at the small 2nd floor balcony

to the left once you enter. There you will find a store offering "Jorodi Masks & Beads". Now sound out "Jorodi", and you'll find it's an audio homage to Joe Rhode. It's clever, isn't it?

But it doesn't end there. Also attached to the balcony railing is a sign that reads "Earrings", which is also a nod to Mr. Rhode and the unique earring he is known for wearing in his left ear.

A Tow Away Zone

While staying at the Hotel Burudika, you'll want to heed this sign in Swahili and leave your livestock somewhere else. Loosely translated, it means *"No Permission to Install Livestock In Front Of This Wall"*.

Did you notice the sign atop the entry to the railcar on the Wildlife Express? It also tells you that no livestock is allowed on the train.

Baloo is Hiding Around the Corner

Now make your way over to Tamu Tamu Refreshments to find an Imagineer's secret that has been skillfully hidden in plain view right in front of guests. There, on a partial wall in the seating area behind the restaurant and near the path to Asia, is a patchwork of

plaster shaped to resemble Baloo, the bear from Disney's popular 1967 animated film, *The Jungle Book*.

Up and to the right of Baloo is a sort of, kind of, possibly, maybe a Hidden Mickey.

FOR SURE A HIDDEN MICKEY

Out on the street, just out from the Hidden Baloo, is a set of two cleanout covers. Take a look at the stones pressed into the cement around one of the covers, and you'll find it's a Hidden Mickey!

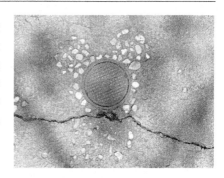

SOUNDS LIKE HARAMBE

While much of the story at Disney's Animal Kingdom is told with visual elements, such as landscaping, architecture, color, perspectives and more, Disney Imagineers have also filled the park with creative sounds, each of which is designed to add to the story. From the distant...and purposely distinct...whistle of the Wildlife Express train to the roar of the Expedition Everest cars as they scream down the mountainside, sound fills the park and completes the magic. However, if guests don't pay attention, much of it will be missed, and that part of the story will remain untold.

Make your way to in front of the Tusker House in Harambe and listen for a while to hear sounds that have been added to help create a sense of the bustle found in the small village. Pause here and listen for the landlady who is banging on a door upstairs trying to get into a room.

Now continue this audio discovery by moving over to the nearby Tusker House Restaurant and listening closely to the sounds of a very busy kitchen emanating from somewhere close by.

A Genuine Pillar Post Box

As you visit Harambe, you'll notice small references to its former rule under the British Empire. The trains that ply the tracks to the Conservation Station were, according to local lore, built in 1926 by the Horwich Works in North West England, the clock found overhead at the train station itself bears the mark *Windsor Royal Station 1897*, and standing to the right of the Harambe Port Authority building one can find a genuine cast iron red pillar post box.

Bearing the crown and royal cypher for King George VI, this post box was installed sometime during his monarchy, which reigned from December of 1936 to February of 1952. The fanciful "R" of the royal cypher on its base refers to "Rex", which is Latin for "King" and the letter "G" is in reference to George, thus King George. This post box is similar to the post box you'll find in the United Kingdom pavilion at Epcot, though that box bears a cypher of "ER", designating Queen Elizabeth II, who began her reign in 1952, following the death of King George VI.

A Harambe Hidden Mickey

Pressed into the cement street just left of the Mombasa Marketplace building is a set of stones arranged around a cleanout cover to form a Hidden Mickey. It may be covered by a vendor's cart, but it's there for you to discover.

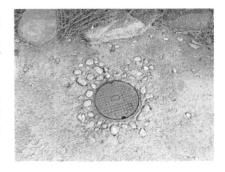

ANOTHER HARAMBE
HIDDEN MICKEY

Over by the Harambe Fruit Market, look on the ground for a large patch of dark pavement set into the stones beneath a collection of tables. There, you'll spot another Harambe Hidden Mickey!

HIDDEN MICKEY

Stepping over by the Harambe Market, you'll see an image of Mickey Mouse painted on a building exterior. Beneath the image it reads *Fichwa! Fellow*. Disney's Animal Kingdom is home to perhaps more Hidden Mickeys than any other park, as evidenced by all those you find in this chapter. From over 100 Hidden Mickeys at the Conservation Station entrance to the Hidden Mickey island in Kilimanjaro Safaris, you can find him hiding everywhere, provided you're looking. It's only fitting that Mickey is portrayed on this wall along with the words *Hidden Fellow* in Swahili!

KILIMANJARO SAFARIS

Kilimanjaro Safaris is an amazing adventure filled with all kinds of African animals, all of which appear in a natural habitat setting, and for many guests, animals such as the lions, elephants, cheetahs and crocodiles are the highlights of the attraction.

Here's what you need to know to get the best view of these magnificent animals. Like most attractions, seating is assigned by a Cast Member once you reach the ride vehicle. The lions, elephants, crocodiles and cheetahs are on the left side of the vehicle as you move through the attraction, so to get the best view during your journey, ask the Cast Member seating guests if you may be seated on the left side of the vehicle, in the back row. This gives you the very best view of all of these animals, and you'll get much better pictures, as well.

Note: The Hippos also tend to be seen on the left side of the vehicle, though not always. The stately giraffes are very mobile throughout the attraction and can be seen on either side.

Tip: Want to get a photo like the one here, with the ride vehicle making the turn while an elephant stands in the background? It takes two things to get it, one you can control, and the other is pure (mostly) luck. When you board the ride vehicle, ask to be seated on the far left side of the very back row. Now, as you make your way through the attraction, have your camera ready once you pass the large Baobab tree, where the elephants gather. Being located in the back seat, you'll have an unobstructed view of the scene after you pass the tree and won't have any other guests' heads in the foreground, as you would if you took this same picture from another seat in the ride vehicle. You'll still have to twist and contort quite a bit to get the shot, but it is worth it for this classic Kilimanjaro Safari photo. As far as the elephant in the background and the ride vehicle behind you making the turn at just the right time?...well, that's the luck part, but the ride vehicles are evenly spaced during the trip, and there is often food left right at the spot in which the elephant is standing, so odds are in your favor.

A HIDDEN MICKEY ISLAND

As the ride vehicle makes its way through the attraction, it passes a large Baobab tree, which is often frequented by elephants. Just beyond the tree is a large pond with a small island inhabited by flamingos. Look closely, and you'll see the shape of the island is actually a Hidden Mickey.

Tip: Visit Google Earth to see this Hidden Mickey in detail.

HEED THIS NEXT SECRET

As you exit Kilimanjaro Safaris, you'll pass a small structure for Warden Post No. 4. On its exterior wall, you'll see the following phrase...

HAKUNA RUHUSA YA KUPITA HAPA
MKUBWA WA HIFADHI PEKE YAKE

In Swahili, it's telling you that you do not have permission to enter the park.

A REVISED HIDDEN MICKEY

Located on the tile countertop of a merchandise cart parked near the entrance to the Gorilla Falls Exploration Trail is a Hidden Mickey that used to be perhaps the second smallest in all of Walt Disney World. Made up of tiny beads, it was set into the tile grout only to be found by those who sought it. Today, that Hidden Mickey has been replaced by another one a bit larger, but it's still not easy to find. Can you find it?

THE SMALLEST & LARGEST HIDDEN MICKEYS IN THE WORLD

Want to find one of the smallest Hidden Mickeys in all of Walt Disney World Resort? Then head to the southwest entrance of the Pizzafari Restaurant and study the large bugs carved onto the shutters of the windows there. Look closely and you'll find one of the smallest Hidden Mickeys in all of Walt Disney World Resort, a title that used to be held by a small beaded Hickey Mickey in a nearby vendor's cart, until it was replaced with a larger one.

The smallest Hidden Mickey at Walt Disney World? That title belongs to the tiny Hidden Mickey found on the shirt of the caricature of Steve Barrett, *The Hidden Mickey Guy*, which can be found on a booth divider panel in the End Zone Food Court in the All Star Sports Resort. Hint: Look for Minnie playing hockey.

The largest Hidden Mickey? That title belongs to a massive solar array shaped like a classic 3-circle Hidden Mickey, which is located outside of Epcot. *Solar array photo copyright Jonathan Salazar.*

THREE MORE HIDDEN MICKEYS

You're not done searching for Hidden Mickeys at the Pizzafari restaurant quite yet! Look for two Hidden Mickeys and one Hidden Mickey set of ears elsewhere in the restaurant. You'll find one in each of the main dining rooms.

YOUR VERY OWN
CLASSIC HIDDEN MICKEY

Now make your way to the nearby Gorilla Falls Nature Trail to help save the planet and maybe an endangered classic Hidden Mickey.

At one point, the Research Station was renovated, and a number of items inside were removed, including the very popular Asepso soap box Hidden Mickey. One of the very first antiseptic soaps, Asepso became widely known overseas in the early 1900s as one of the first soaps to alleviate infections and reduce bacteria on the skin, but perhaps more importantly, it also cooled the skin and alleviated the effects of prickly heat in tropical climate locales, such as the Pangani Forest.

By using Asepso soap instead of a more generic American brand, Disney Imagineers had used a simple and very small prop to further immerse guests in the story that is the Gorilla Falls Nature Trail. And by adding two small circles to the front of the box, they created a whimsical...and classic...Hidden Mickey.

Unfortunately, this small box is now no longer part of the Research Station, no doubt because it would often go missing and, as a result, need frequent replacing. So how can we perhaps help bring about its return? By encouraging guests to make their own Asepso soap box Hidden Mickey souvenir! Simply go online to order a box, which may need to come from overseas. Once it arrives, apply a couple of round white stickers in a manner similar to the image above and you'll have your very own classic Disney's Animal Kingdom Hidden Mickey! Note that there are a number of different designs for the front of the box, some of which are similar but not the same as that which appears on the prior page.

HIDDEN MICKEY FLAP

While you're in the Research Station, find the backpack hanging on the wall and take note of the corner of the outer flap. Do you see the Hidden Mickey, next to the strap? *Photo courtesy of WDWGuidedTours.com.*

WILDLIFE EXPRESS TRAIN

The Wildlife Express Train is a narrow gauge train powered by a British steam engine, which as the *story* goes, was manufactured for Beyer, Peacock & Company in 1926. As you walk about Disney's Animal Kingdom, listen carefully to the distant sound of the train's steam whistle. Notice anything different about it? Unlike the more robust sound of the "American train whistles" at the Magic Kingdom, the Imagineers made sure this whistle blasts with the higher shrill of a British steam engine, so as to ensure the accuracy of the story.

AN IDEA TRANSPORTED FROM DISNEYLAND

Now as you journey aboard the Wildlife Express Train, note that the seats are actually benches which all face the same way.

Believe it or not, but this design ties back to a discovery made over 65 years ago, in the early days of Disneyland.

The first Disneyland Railroad cars were designed like any other in the country at that time. Guests would enter through the ends of the cars and walk down a center aisle with seats on each side, but disembarking from such a configuration takes a good deal of time and can be an exercise in frustration. In addition, it can keep the trains from running on time. Disney Imagineers soon realized that guests could more easily...and more quickly...board and disembark from the train if they could access the rail car from large openings on the side, instead of from a single doorway on each end. This design efficiency developed in Disneyland is now perfected today in the Wildlife Express Train 3,000 miles away!

CONSERVE THIS
HIDDEN MICKEY

Once at the Conservation Station, find the set of three Petri dishes placed on a window sill to form a Hidden Mickey. In addition to whimsical secrets like this, the Conservation Station is an excellent opportunity for children of all ages to interact

with small animals, including goats, sheep, donkeys, and pigs, as well as see live giant toads, lizards, tarantulas, snakes, and even Komodo dragons.

Over 100
Hidden Mickeys in One Place!

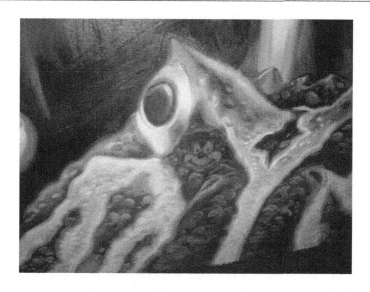

You walked right past them, didn't you? Make the mistake of joining the multitudes who hurry past the entrance mural at the Conservation Station, and you'll pass up a delightful and engaging hour of fun for the whole family! As you enter or leave the Conservation Station, stop to study the large mural on each side of the entrance hallway. Look closely, and you'll find countless Hidden Mickeys mixed in with the animal

images, with Mickey hidden in the spots of a butterfly's wing, the iris of an Ostrich's eye, the skin of a frog, and many, many more. Can you see Mickey's face in the photo above?

WILDLIFE EXPRESS
TRAIN STATION

The authentic architecture of the train station for the Wildlife Express Train reflects the elements typically found in the railroad stations of East Africa during the early 1900s.

A TRIBUTE TO BOB HARPUR

Disney Imagineers are honored all throughout Walt Disney World Resort, and if you look carefully at Engine 02594 of the Wildlife Express, you'll find the name of R. Baba Harpoor, a nod to Disney Imagineer Bob Harpur. Mr. Harpur not only shared an interest in miniature trains with Walt Disney, but he also played a key role in acquiring and restoring the locomotives in use at Walt Disney World Resort today.

DiVine

Think all green leafy plants are the same? You may find out otherwise when you enter Disney's Animal Kingdom.

Unsuspecting guests walking between Africa and Asia are often surprised by DiVine, a tall walking plant on stilts which emerges from hiding in plain sight amidst the foliage to delight guests, usually with a bit of surprise. Note that DiVine can be very difficult to spot, even though she may be right before your eyes. Standing on tall stilts and completely covered in ivy-like foliage, she may wrap herself around a tree, drape herself on a building or simply stand next to the trail, all while being perfectly camouflaged... until she starts moving. Note: As with Disney characters, DiVine appears on occasion and only for a while, so she is not always in the park. In addition, she may appear in The Oasis at times.

DiVine photo courtesy of Aaron DelPrince

YOU'LL WANT THE PATH LESS TRAVELED

As you walk from Africa to Asia, you may choose one of two paths. One is wide and busy, but disappearing into the jungle is a quieter narrower path that offers not only less traffic, but also beautiful views of the Tree of Life and a quiet place to sit, mixed with a possible opportunity to meet a Disney character along the way.

A "Secret" Viewpoint

You'll notice that those guests taking the busier pathway between Africa and Asia often miss a small side path that winds its way down to the river and a small stone patio, which offers a very nice view of the Tree of Life. You'll find this unmarked pathway just a bit east of Harambe. Take the turn, follow the trail, and enjoy your reward!

Charged for a Bottle of Coke

Here's a fun-to-discover secret the Disney Imagineers have placed as a creative story element, which guests just might find in a small Asian village. Just out from the entrance to the Kali River Rapids ride is a tall utility pole strung with all kinds of wires, lights, insulators and more. Mixed in with that collection is an old Coke bottle, which, being made of glass, has been inverted and turned into an insulator.

KALI RIVER RAPIDS

Ride interaction is a somewhat rare opportunity at Walt Disney World, but this next secret reveals a fun way to interact with guests on Kali River Rapids.

As you exit the attraction and make your way across the bridge that spans the Kali River, look for two small control panels placed on the right railing. These panels hold buttons which control the two ornately decorated elephants below, and pushing them causes a stream of water to squirt from the elephant's trunks onto unsuspecting guests in the rafts as they drift past.

MY FAVORITE HIDDEN MICKEY

There are hundreds of Hidden Mickeys scattered all throughout Walt Disney World Resort, and of those, this one is my favorite. Stop in front of Gupta's Gear near Expedition Everest and study the mountaineering equipment attached to the posts and

tucked up underneath the roof. Near the left hand side, out on the main walkway, you'll spot two rings and a bit of cord that together creates a familiar, yet always overlooked, shape.

A "GRATE" HIDDEN MICKEY

Now step to your left, over by the pile of bricks, and you'll find a collection of grates stacked against the wall. Do you see the Hidden Mickey in the ironwork?

MT. EVEREST UP CLOSE

As you approach Mt. Everest from Africa, be on the lookout for a telescope. Sometimes obscured by guests taking photos at this photo spot, the telescope offers an up close view of the upper reaches of the mountain, as well as the riders screaming with excitement on Expedition Everest.

EXPEDITION EVEREST

This next secret is an amazing display of the Imagineers' use of ride technology, which most guests miss because they are purposely distracted. As your train begins its harrowing journey high on the mountain, it careens around a corner before coming to a halt only a few feet away from a section of broken track hanging over a terrifying drop. Pausing for only a moment, it then begins to plummet backwards down the mountain and into the darkness before coming to a halt once again. Here's where you'll want to pay attention.

While the animated Yeti menace appears on a screen with a terrifying roar, look away and peer toward the opening straight ahead. There you will see an entire stretch of track "flip" over in preparation of sending you  screaming into the void and down the mountainside!

A HIDDEN MICKEY EXPEDITION

The queue lines for Expedition Everest are filled with artifacts from the expeditions that have preceded yours. Packs, crampons, ropes, boots, ice axes, and much more are placed on display or hung from the rafters above. Among these items, you'll also find two lanterns, both of which display a familiar set of dents in their bases, one of which appears to have been caused by a rampaging yeti!

AN ANCIENT LOCK

Also found in the queue for Expedition Everest are ancient cultural artifacts. As you make your way through, you'll notice an  interesting looking contraption secured above a doorway. Given its unconventional shape, by today's standards it's not readily apparent as to what this is, but it's actually an ancient lock used by the Nepalese to secure the heavy double doors of a Hindu temple.

ABOUT THAT YETI

The fur on the fearsome yeti is a mix of yak fur, horse hair and synthetics, with a touch of Spanish moss thrown in for good measure.

According to the Disney Archives, the Yeti in Expedition Everest is the single most powerful Audio-Animatronic figure in use in Disney parks. The tallest?...That would be the Fantasmic dragon. And the smallest?...Chef Remy at the France pavilion in the World Showcase at Epcot.

HIMALAYAN HIDDEN MICKEY

As you exit the Expedition Everest attraction, you'll pass through a gift shop offering wares from high in the Himalaya. Take note of a flower painted above a set of shelves, and you'll spot a Himalayan Hidden Mickey in its petals.

DINOLAND, U.S.A.

Now travel to Dinoland U.S.A. and find the Highway 498 sign located over by Primeval Whirl. Appearing to be simply a random design element, it actually ties in with three other "signs" scattered throughout all four parks, all of which denote the year the park opened. The Magic Kingdom opened in 1971, as indicated by Fire Station 71 in the Town Square, Epcot opened in 1982, as shown on the farmhouse mailbox of The Land, Disney's  Hollywood Studios opened in 1989, as indicated on the gas pumps of Oscar's Super Service gas station and Disney's Animal Kingdom opened on April 22, 1998, hence "Hwy 498."

AN OUT OF THIS WORLD HIDDEN MICKEY

The large colorful sign for Primeval Whirl depicts the pending demise of the dinosaurs as a fiery asteroid plummets toward the earth. Hidden amongst the asteroid's iron, nickel, magnesium, silicon, and gold is another valuable element...a Hidden Mickey. Can you find it?

A Paved Hidden Mickey

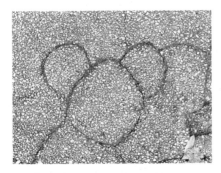

Themed paving is an important element used all throughout Disney's parks. The impressions of horseshoes can be found by the Haunted Mansion in the Magic Kingdom, droid tracks can be found throughout Star Wars Land, Yeti prints can be found by Mt. Everest, and even cracks formed over the decades can be found in the pavement at Chester & Hester's Dino-Rama. Take a look at the cracks in the pavement opposite the south entrance to Chester & Hester's Dino-Rama and you'll find the Imagineers had a little fun in creating a Hidden Mickey.

Cretaceous Trail

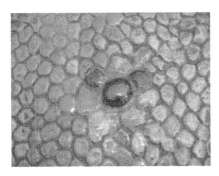

Tucked out of the mainstream is the quiet Cretaceous Trail, a wide pathway designed to allow young children to trek through and learn about the world of dinosaurs...and perfect for parents to take a quiet break. As you walk the trail, keep an eye out for a large duck-billed Corythosaurus resting on the ground. Here, among the scales on its back, you'll find a Hidden Mickey over 77 million years old! Before you say goodbye to this denizen of the Upper Cretaceous Period, be sure to take a look at the scarf around its neck. Can you spot another Hidden Mickey?

AN ANCIENT HIDDEN MICKEY

Study the large murals you see as you enter the DINOSAUR attraction to find two ancient Hidden Mickeys. On your right as you enter, you'll find a mural with a tree on the left hand side. Notice where a branch connects to the trunk and you'll find a classic three-circle Hidden Mickey. Across the way, you'll see a mural with a depiction of an explosion. Take a look amidst the chaos for another Hidden Mickey there.

IMAGINEERING WHIMSY

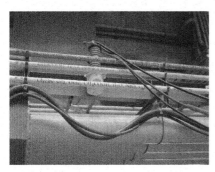

Disney Imagineers are a serious bunch, but they definitely have a whimsical side, as well. As you descend the stairs in the DINOSAUR ride vehicle staging area, notice the three pipes to the left colored red, yellow and white. The chemical compounds displayed here are for. . . ketchup, mustard and mayonnaise!

YES U IS

Outside the entrance to the Restaurantosaurus, you'll find a vintage Airstream trailer with a sign that reads "I ARE SMART". This is a fun anagram of AIRSTREAM, placed here by one of the paleontology students.

AN AMERICAN CROCODILE

The American Crocodiles of the Kilimanjaro Safaris attraction are impressive, but they are seen at a distance from the ride vehicle. This next secret reveals the whereabouts of an American Crocodile that is not only impressive in size, but also viewed from a much closer perspective. It is perhaps the closest you will ever come to a crocodile of this size, and most guests pass by without ever noticing it is there.

As you make your way toward Restaurantosaurus, stop and peer over the edge of the American Crocodile exhibit across from the restaurant. There, in the small pond, you will see a creature of gargantuan size only a few feet away. While often resting, keep an eye on it as it does periodically move.

BTW, how real is the Discovery River? So real that live alligators sometimes find their way in for a swim. Here is a photo I took of a young alligator swimming in the river between Asia and Africa.

A QUIET VIEW OF MT. EVEREST

Disney's Animal Kingdom is usually quite busy, as guests travel the world from Africa to Asia, as well as back and forth through time from Dino-Land to Pandora. If you'd like to step away from this hustle and bustle to find a quiet spot to take in beautiful views of Mt. Everest across the water, then find your way to the paths and tables behind the Flame Tree Barbecue. Here, you'll find fewer guests, a tranquil water feature, perhaps a stately white egret or ibis, and scenic views perfect for enjoying a slower pace for a while.

MAHARAJAH HIDDEN MICKEYS

There are a number of Hidden Mickeys dispersed along the Maharajah Jungle Trek. Here are a few for you to discover while you journey along...As you make your way through the Anandapur Royal Forest into a collection of ruins, look for a painting of one of the four kings hunting with a bow and arrow, and take note of his right ear. Exiting the ruins, look to your left on the last wall to find a group of leaves, three of which conveniently hide the treasure you seek. Next, find a viewing area for the tigers. To the right is a bundle of sticks atop a crate, three of which clearly form a familiar shape.

A MAGICAL FOUNTAIN

After exiting the Maharajah Jungle Trek, you'll find to your right two small buildings, one of which holds a rather unique and intriguing fountain. Unlike a typical fountain that spews a stream of water, this one disperses water from its top in the shape of an unbroken liquid dome. Stop for a moment here to enjoy this magical fountain.

MIND THE BAJA TICKLER

As you enter Pandora – The World of Avatar, you'll quickly realize that this is a world of dense and exotic foliage containing plants unlike anything you've ever seen on earth. One of the most important plants you'll discover here is the large Baja Tickler, also known as *txumtsa'wll*, meaning "poison-squirting plant". Appearing similar to an oversized ear of corn growing at an angle, its existence is vital for the survival of the population of Pandora, for it spends its life absorbing the toxic gases found in the moon's atmosphere and consolidating them into a watery mix within its core. Once this liquid builds up enough pressure, the plant then periodically expels it as a toxic plume from its thorny top. You'll find a Baja Tickler on your right as you enter Pandora from Discovery Island. If the pathway is wet when you approach it, then that means the plant is spewing its toxic liquid, so you'll want to avoid it...or consider running through it and having fun with the kids!

RELICS OF THE WAR

A little ways beyond the Baja Tickler, you'll notice a couple of old relics from the war rusting in the foliage, well off the trail. They're very difficult to spot, since they blend right in, but on your right, just beyond the small stream, are the remains of a

Scorpion helicopter, while on your left is what appears to be a transport covered in rust.

You Were Warned

Make your way to a small pond with cascading water at a viewing platform for the floating mountains. There, you will find a collection of shelled animals floating on the surface. Study them closely, as they are rather interesting looking, but do not get too close, as a nearby sign warns...

BE AWARE! This pond contains animals that shoot powerful jets of water into the air to hunt small flying creatures. Sudden arm movements close to the pond may trigger this hunting response. YOU MAY GET WET!

AMP & Pandora Utility Suit

Towering in front of Pongu Pongu is a menacing looking Amplified Mobility Platform (AMP), or Exosuit. Used in the war, today it has been rendered useless by the Na'vi and is staged here as a reminder of the past. Look closely at its many joints and you'll find they've all been welded so as to make sure the suit can never again be used to fight.

Similar to the AMP is the fully functional Pandora Utility Suit. Standing 10' tall, it is piloted by a human and is used to explore the Mo'ara Valley, collect plant samples, study Pandora, and interact with guests. You'll often find it by the AMP, or elsewhere within the park, so keep an eye out for it.

TAGS, THEY'RE IT!

While getting a refreshing drink at Pongu Pongu, take note of the collection of dog tags hanging up above from the rafters. The faces you see here are the Imagineers who created Pandora – The World of Avatar, with Joe Rhode placed top and center.

YOU'RE NOT FROM AROUND HERE, ARE YOU?

When speaking with Cast Members while in Pandora, take note of their name tags. You'll find that in addition to their hometown and state, it also lists what planet they're from.

PANDORA CREATURE TRACKS

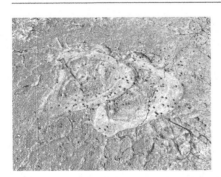

You're not alone while trekking through Pandora. Note how the Imagineers have themed the pavement with the tracks of a Direhorse, as well as a dreaded Thanator.

www.Disney-Secrets.com

FORCED PERSPECTIVE
WITH WATER

The Imagineer's use of forced perspective throughout the parks of Walt Disney World is legendary. From Cinderella Castle and the buildings of Main Street, U.S.A. to the Hollywood Tower of Terror and the towering ancient temple in Epcot's Mexico pavilion, we are constantly being "tricked" into believing less is more as part of the story.

As you make your way along the queue for Avatar, visually follow the different waterfalls back up into the mountains and you'll see near the top the highest waterfall that begins them all. Here, the Imagineers were faced with a problem. They recognized that water that falls at a distance displays different characteristics than water that falls nearby, so if they simply created a small waterfall here, then the look of the falling water would be incongruent with the forced perspective of the "distant" mountains they had created all around it. As a result, they "manipulated" the water such that it is not real water at all, but instead a material that resembles water moving on a vertical conveyor belt-like loop.

FLAKY DETAIL

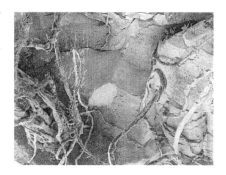

So much of the story of Pandora – The World of Avatar is told in the smallest of details. The welds on the AMD, the name of their home planet on Cast Members' name tags, and in this case, a geological occurrence that conveys the realism of the floating mountains. Stand under this impressive icon of Pandora and look at its underside. There, you will see lighter sections of rock which indicate that portions have recently flaked away, just as they would with mountains that had formed eons ago.

PANDORA BIOLUMINESCENCE

Visit Pandora only during the daytime hours and you're sure to miss out on this next secret. Once the sun goes down, the plants, animals, mountains, pathways, and even the water comes to life in a spectacle of bioluminescent colors making for a truly memorable experience.

THREE GUIDING PRINCIPLES

"Animal Kingdom is built around these three values; Intrinsic value of nature, psychological transformation of a person through extraordinary adventure, and a personal call to action." – Disney Imagineer Joe Rhode

A WDW Guided Tours Tip:

There is a "secret" unmarked front-row queue at Expedition Everest. Simply tell the ride attendant that you'd like to ride in the front seats of the train, and they will direct you to the special front row queue.

Courtesy of WDWGuidedTours.com

THANK YOU!

I hope you have enjoyed this journey through the secrets & stories of Walt Disney World as much as I've enjoyed sharing them with you. Remember, there are many more secrets which you'll walk past, over and through as you explore the ever-changing magic of the parks. Where there is nothing today, there may be a new classic tomorrow just waiting to be revealed.

Enjoy discovering the magic!

Mike Fox

THE HIDDEN SECRETS & STORIES OF DISNEYLAND

"Almost every page contained details I had never noticed before."
– Disney Legend Bob Gurr

If you enjoyed reading these secrets about Walt Disney World, then you're sure to enjoy *The Hidden Secrets & Stories of Disneyland*. The companion book to this title, it is a fun and entertaining look at **over 250** of the magical secrets and story elements purposely hidden by the Disney Imagineers throughout Disneyland...all arranged as a fun tour and complete with **more than 220** photos!

Available online and at select retailers. Learn more at:

www.Disney-Secrets.com

DISNEYLAND IN-DEPTH

In Depth Details Behind the
Magical Story Elements of Disneyland

Disneyland In-Depth reveals 46 fascinating in-depth backstories behind the magical story elements found throughout Disneyland. Within its pages, you'll learn about *The Disneyland News* - the monthly newspaper sold on Opening Day in 1955, the innovative 1914 film that inspired a young 12 year-old Walt Disney to become an animator, the *complete* story behind the creation of the very first Hidden Mickey, the restoration of Walt's beloved Lilly Belle Steam Engine, the now rare book Walt used to learn how to draw Mickey Mouse, the small advertisement Walt would place in magazines for a 35 cent catalog he was selling...while at the height of his career, and much more, *including many stories that have never before been published in any Disney-related books, articles or web sites!* Available online and select retailers. Learn more at:

www.Disney-Secrets.com

Acknowledgments

Many people have graciously contributed to the development of this book. From Michael Broggie's biography of his father and Disney Legend, Roger Broggie, and Jeff Baham's exclusive story about the attic scene in Disneyland's Haunted Mansion, to the Disney Archive's providing a key date for solving a puzzling timeline, and Dave Drumheller's big help in obtaining last-minute photos, many have played a role, large or small, in helping me write a title which contains not only quality content, but also family value entertainment that is respectful of the legacy of Walt Disney.

For that, I would like to thank you all...

- Barry Snyder – Walt Disney Imagineering
- Beth Green – ADisneyMom'sThoughts.com
- Bob Gurr – Disney Legend and Imagineer
- Brian Hillman – George H. Lloyd Relative
- Brian Hull – Voice Impressionist/Singer/Composer
- Carrie Hayward – DisneyTravelBabble.com
- Chip Confer – ChipandCo.com
- Cindy Bothner – Walt Disney Imagineering
- Dave DeCaro – Davelandweb.com
- Dave Drumheller – WDWGuidedTours.com
- David Leaphart – SteelWheelonSteelRail.com
- David Lesjak – Disney Historian
- Disneyana Fan Club – Cascade Chapter
- Doobie Moseley – LaughingPlace.com
- Doug Leonard – Walt Disney Imagineering
- Frank Reifsnyder – Walt Disney Imagineering
- George Eldridge – Decoding the Disneyland Telegraph
- Glenn Barker – Walt Disney Imagineering

- Jack Ferencin - Hellertown, PA
- Jeff Baham - DoomBuggies.com
- Jeff Kober - PerformanceJourneys.com
- Jenn Lissak - DisneyBabiesBlog.com
- Jim Korkis - Disney Historian
- Jason Dziegielewski- DisneyGeek.com
- Jordan Sallis - George H. Lloyd Relative
- Marty Sklar - Disney Legend and Imagineer
- Michael & Sharon Broggie - Disney Historians
- Michael Campbell - President, Carolwood Pacific Historical Society
- Mike Ellis - MyDreamsofDisney.com
- Mike Westby - Disney App & Guidebook Author
- Mousestalgia.com Podcast
- Ray Kinman - Walt Disney Imagineering
- Steve DeGaetano - Disneyland Railroad Historian - SteamPassages.com
- Tammy Benson - Golden Spike NHS
- Terry Peterson - Walt Disney Imagineering
- The Disney Archives

And most of all my parents, Richard & Roberta, for taking me to Disneyland for the very first time many years ago!

SELECTED BIBLIOGRAPHY

Many sources of content, including interviews, books, articles, documents, vintage publications, photos, correspondence, video and of course countless theme park visits were used in the research for this book.

Here are some publications which were not only helpful, but I would highly recommend them as reading material for anyone interested in Walt Disney World, Disneyland or Disney history...

Baham, Jeff. *The Unauthorized Story of Walt Disney's Haunted Mansion.* Theme Park Press, 2014

Bain, David Haward. *Empire Express: Building the First Transcontinental Railroad.* Penguin Books, 2000

Berg, Walter G. *Buildings and Structures of American Railroads.* 1893

Broggie, Michael. *Walt Disney's Railroad Story.* Donning Company Publishers, 4th Edition. 2014

DeGaetano, Steve. *The Disneyland Railroad – A Complete History in Words and Pictures.* 1st Edition. 2015

Gabler, Neal. *Walt Disney: The Triumph of the American Imagination.* Alfred A. Knopf, 2006

Kober, J. Jeff. *Disneyland at Work.* Performance Journeys, 2010

Kober, J. Jeff. *Disney's Hollywood Studios – From Show Biz to Your Biz.* Theme Park Press, 2014

Lloyd, George. *George H. Lloyd's Hand Carved Caenstone Model of Our National Capitol.* Lowenstein's, Approx. 1943

Sklar, Marty. *Dream It! Do It!: My Half-Century Creating Disney's Magic Kingdoms.* Disney Editions, 2013

Smith, Dave. *Disney A to Z: The Updated Official Encyclopedia.* Disney Editions, 1998

Strodder, Chris. *The Disneyland Encyclopedia.* Santa Monica Press, 2012

The Philadelphia Contributionship Digital Archives – Philadelphiabuildings.org

Thomas, Bob. *Walt Disney: An American Original.* Hyperion, 1994

Van Eaton, Mike. *Van Eaton Galleries Presents the story of Disneyland – an exhibition and sale catalog.* 2015

Wright, Alex and The Imagineers: *The Imagineering Field Guide to Disneyland.* Disney Editions, 2008

Wright, Alex and The Imagineers: *The Imagineering Field Guide to Epcot.* Disney Editions, 2006

Wright, Alex and The Imagineers. *The Imagineering Field Guide to The Magic Kingdom.* Disney Editions, 2005

www.Disney-Secrets.com